THE American DINER

MICHAEL KARL WITZEL

MBI Publishing Company

DEDICATION

I dedicate *The American Diner* to my gourmand parents, Gabriele and Karl Witzel, who transported me in a variety of automobiles to roadside food joints located all over the state of New Jersey. Frequently we took our place at the counter of the White Castle, and when we were in a hurry, bought 'em by the sack and wolfed them down right in the car. Sometimes my mom escorted me to exotic eateries like the quaint little lunch counter at the W. T. Grant outlet in Pompton Lakes, where I perched high atop a gleaming, rotating diner stool, spinning about with glee until motion sickness and the sight of mouth-watering hot dogs (grilling and turning on heated rollers) commanded my attention. My dad was one of the original road-food junkies and, as a direct consequence, introduced me to a host of memorable diners and lunch counters. Along the highways designated by the state as Route 23 and 46, we zigzagged through the traffic and chased the neon lights to sample our favorite diner haute cuisine. Great diner eateries such as the Spindletop, Silver Dollar Diner, Short Stop, Fair Lynne, Chuck-Hut, Tick-Tock, and White Manna (and many, many more) are all a part of my memory now—a rich resource of vivid sights, sounds, tastes, and smells that transport me back to a time when eating away from home was still a great adventure.

First published in 1999 by MBI Publishing Company, 729 Prospect Avenue, PO Box 1, Osceola, WI 54020-0001USA

© Michael Karl Witzel, 1999

MBI Publishing Company books are also available at discounts in bulk quantity for industrial or sales-promotional use. For details write to Special Sales Manager at Motorbooks International Wholesalers & Distributors, 729 Prospect Avenue, PO Box 1, Osceola WI, 54020 USA.

Library of Congress Cataloging-in-Publication Data

Witzel, Michael Karl.
    The American diner / Michael Karl Witzel.
        p. cm.
    Includes index.
    ISBN 0-7603-0110-7 (hardbound : alk. paper)
    1. Diners (Restaurants–United States–History. I. Title.
  TX945.W57   1998
  647.9573'09–dc21   98-49601

Edited by Michael Dapper
Designed by Tom Heffron

Printed in China through World Print, Ltd.

On the front cover: Johnny D's diner is one of the new Kullman breed. Owned by John Daskalis and doing business in New Windsor, New York, it features porcelain fluted panels and colorful Spandrel glass (used for its great reflective quality) as important design elements. *Courtesy of Kullman Industries*

On the frontispiece: In Houston, Texas, Simpson's Diner exists as undeniable proof that the diner has made it South of the Mason-Dixon line. *Courtesy Roadway Express/John Puglia*

On the title page: Earl Rees operated the Ingleside Diner for more years than people can remember. Back in 1996, he retired from the business and sold the popular Thorndale, Pennsylvania, eatery to a company called Food Masters of Raleigh, North Carolina. With its dramatic corner entrance, bold use of neon, and stainless steel, this giant Fodero is sure to "keep on keepin' on!" *Ronald Saari ©1999*

On the preface page: The Penn Diner took much of its beauty from the curved strips of bare and porcelain-enameled metal running in vertical lengths around its periphery. It's interesting to note that before the days of modern fast food, a diner's name wasn't as important as the food. If you found a place that claimed it was a "Good Place to Eat," that was all you needed. *Preziosi Postcards*

On the back cover: *Top:* An air conditioned beauty located near Philadelphia on U.S. Route 30, Jim and Bill's Mari-Nay is typical of the porcelain panel-and-stainless steel diners made by a number of diner manufacturers. *Courtesy Roger Jackson*

Inset: Pal's Diner continues to offer the same sort of popular diner fare as it originally did when it was located in Mahwah, New Jersey. While regional specialties often define the realm of dinerdom, customers expect simple comfort foods prepared and served without pomp and circumstance. *Courtesy Barry Brown*

Bottom: What's more inviting? A cozy row of diner stools or the plastic booth found at the local fast food outlet? *Jonathan Yonan ©1999*

THE AMERICAN DINER

TABLE NO.	NO. PERSONS	CHECK NO.	SERVER NO.
		702837	

CONTENTS

TAX

REORDER #4805909

The American diner is an institution that has managed to stay alive through many changes in building styles and trends, not to mention the general public's tastes, whims, and attitudes toward eating out. From its beginnings as a horse-drawn lunch wagon in the 1870s (serving factory workers and other late-night habitué) to the mega-restaurants of the 1990s (serving city dwellers and travelers along the highways and byways of America, in most cases 24 hours a day), the diner has continued to win the hearts of Americans eating on the go.

Since 1980, I have been conducting my own travels—what I call a personal research project of documenting existing diners. In the process, I have learned of their history and been able to familiarize myself with the different styles and manufacturers.

I have come to realize that I am not alone out there in my endeavors. There is a subculture of enthusiasts who for various reasons have been drawn to diners, whether out of a sense of nostalgia, history, community, or just in search of a good, home-cooked meal. Indirectly, these enthusiasts have helped diners stay alive. At the same time, this subculture has brought the art of collecting "diner memorabilia" to a whole new level. As my own diner collection would attest, the list of cool collectibles is endless: matchbooks, menus, postcards, T-shirts, and more.

Growing up in the metropolitan Boston area during the 1950s and 1960s, I have a great recollection of the many diners that were still around at that time. I remember having breakfast with my father at places such as the Star Lite Diner and Bobbie's Diner (long since gone), both in my hometown of Medford, as well as the Victoria Diner of Boston (still alive and well).

My mind often wanders back to those Easter Sunday breakfasts at Carroll's Colonial Dining Car with my family after church. A few years later—during the 1970s—I could often be found hanging out at Carroll's with a bunch of my friends. Carroll's was the last diner to survive in Medford (demolished in 1987). Sitting at the counter or in a booth, I recall my own sense of feeling right at home at these diners, playing some tunes on the jukebox and kibitzing with the grill cooks, waitresses, or other patrons. When they disappeared, you can only imagine the feelings of loss!

With a long and interesting history, this unique family-style restaurant known as the diner began its gradual decline from the late 1950s to the early 1980s. From an estimated high of almost 6,000 diners operating during the heyday of the late 1950s to the current 2,000-plus now holding—and inching upward in the 1990s—the diner thrives primarily in the Northeast region of the country. And thanks to the major media exposure seen during the last two decades, diner-style restaurants have made tremendous inroads in previously diner-poor areas such as the West and Southwest.

Although by true definition a diner is usually a factory-built (pre-fabricated) restaurant, a local hole-in-the-wall lunch counter such as Jelly Beans Deli & Diner in Owensboro, Kentucky, certainly fits the bill in all the other criteria: good food, atmosphere, and camaraderie—with a counter, stools, and booths. The match of favorable diner elements is so good that I believe we should stretch the textbook definition of a diner to include other, equally satisfying, built-on-site, local establishments.

Through the pages of his numerous books on roadside and car-culture–related subjects, author Michael Karl Witzel has taken us on an incredible journey. From gasoline service stations to drive-in restaurants, to driving down Route 66 and cruisin' the strip, we've witnessed a slice of America that's disappearing all too fast. It's only natural that he continue this nostalgic time trip by presenting the roadside enthusiast with an eclectic overview of the history, culture, and resurgence in the popularity of diners and how it all fits in with his own vision of growing up in the mid-to-late 20th century. So pick your favorite stool or table, drop a quarter into the slot, punch up your favorite song, and enjoy this entertaining slice of *The American Diner.*

Larry Cultrera
Diner historian and editor:
Diner Hotline, Society for
Commercial Archeology Journal

ACKNOWLEDGMENTS

A hot cup of thank you is poured for all those who took the time and effort to assist with this book, including Howard Ande, Warren Anderson, Kent Bash, Keith Baum, Monica Bessette, Brian Butko, Pat Chapel, Steve Cohen, Larry Collier, Larry Cultrera, Michael Dregni, Michael Dunlavey, Margot Geist, Shellee Graham, Richard Hailey, Dan Harlow, O. B. Hill, Glen Icanberry, Roger Jackson, Pete Jensen, Joan Johnson, Harvey Kaplan, Guy Kudlemyer, Philip Langdon, Marty Lineen Jr., Pedar Ness, James Parker, Ken Parker, Mike Prero, Don Preziosi, Mike Roberson, Allen Rose, Ron Saari, Larry Schulz, Mary Shelly, Mary Tuthill, Dave Wallen, Mike Wallen, Gabriele Witzel, Kristine Witzel, and Jonathan Yonan. Many working diners and companies gave freely of their time and materials, including Al Sloan of Al's Diner; Deborah Griffin and Carol George of the Boulevard Diner; Andre O'Conner of Brint's Diner; John Scheele of Cindy's Diner; John Touhey, Patty Lowry, and Cathy Dickson of the Cutchogue Diner; David Bernstein of Diner Concepts Inc.; Steve Harwin and Diversified Diners Inc.; Ken Higginbotham of the 5 & Diner Franchise Corporation; Brian Harms, Linda Keefe, and Cindy Pawlcyn of Real Restaurants Fog City Diner; Ivan Leshinsky of the Chesapeake Center for Youth Development Inc., a.k.a. the Hollywood Diner; Wayne King of Jimmie's Diner; Christopher Carvell of Kullman Industries; Richard Lloyd of Lloyd's Diner; Miles Henry of the Maine Diner; Deborah Mulholland of the Mayfair Diner; Brooks Bollman of Measured Marketing and the Radio Diner; Steven Weiss, Gabriel Mendez, and Donald Wagstaff of Mels Drive-In; Nancy Garton of the Miss Adams Diner; Barry Brown, and Sam Choi Brown of Pal's Diner; Mary White of Pit's Barbecue Stand; Elizabeth Strebel of the Riverhead Grill Inc.; John Puglia and Roadway Express; Jerry Berta, Madeline Kaczmarczyk, and Fred Tiensivu of Rosie's Diner; Coy Ramsey of Simpson's Diner; Robert Giaimo, Ype Von Hengst, and Chelle Shapleigh of the Silver Diner; and Katy Kelley of White Castle System.

Historical societies and libraries are represented by the Atlanta Historical Society, Texas/Dallas History and Archives Division of the Dallas Public Library, Henry Ford Museum and Greenfield Village, the Historical Society of Western Pennsylvania, Atwater Kent Museum, Library of Congress American Memory Collection, Ken Turino and the Lynn Historical Society, the National Archives, Jennifer Sanborn at the Rhode Island Historical Society, the Security Pacific National Bank Collection/Los Angeles Public Library, the Wichita Public Library, Theresa Davitt of the Worcester Historical Museum, and Nancy Gaudette of the Worcester Public Library.

Additional gratitude is extended to Archival Research International, Karl Klaus at CoolStock; the E. B. Luce Corporation; Bob Cosenza and the Kobal Collection; Douglas Photographics; Imagers; Howard Frank of Personality Photos; Photosource International; Joe De Gennaro of the Rathkamp Matchcover Society; R. C. S. Photography; Sally Moore of Roadrunner Travel Stock; Betts Anderson and Carol Prange of Unicorn Stock Photos; and the University of Louisville Photographic Archives.

Finally, appreciative thanks go to my wife, Gyvel Young-Witzel, for assisting in the preparation, research, and writing of this book—most notably the authorship of the diner sidebars that follow.

—*Michael Karl Witzel*

Defining the Diner Domain

These days, there's a lot of heated debate on the subject of what really is a diner and what isn't. With elbows on the counter (and a strong cup of coffee within reach) sit the dedicated and well-intentioned purists, those present-day diner aficionados and self-described roadside archeologists who view the American restaurant form that's called "diner" as a roadside icon. For many of these salt-and-pepper sages, there are no gray areas when it comes to the physical manifestation of their palate's affection. For them, a diner must be a specific arrangement of roadside architecture—a sanctified, hallowed, commercial institution that has validity only if it boasts a prefabricated lineage born of a factory.

Within this category one finds the classic diner structures exemplified by respected industry manufacturers such as Worcester, Tierney, Fodero, Manno, Bixler, Valentine, J. G. Brill, Mountain View, Kullman, DeRaffele, Jerry O'Mahony, Silk City, Paramount, Swingle, and others. Of course, all these names came to life as distinct, self-contained units in a factory. Workers assembled the majority of their interiors, exteriors, and structures ahead of time. A truck or a train hauled them to their intended site of business, where owners connected them to plumbing and utility lines and opened for business. All the proprietor had to do was add the utensils and foodstuffs and hire on a cigar-chomping cook.

These portable eateries feature at least one or more of the standard interior and exterior components characteristic of the diner stereotype. One of the most important elements is that the overall design and layout of the dining building follows the lead of a train car (short or stretched). Regarding the roof, only a barrel-style cover or monitor treatment qualifies. At the same time, it's important that the building feature a preponderance of windows and a generous application of stainless steel or porcelain-clad panel. Preferred details include a Formica counter, private dining booths, pedestal-style stools, table-top jukeboxes, and a dramatic application of neon lights. Throw in a heavy-duty coffee urn and a waitress named Velma, and the scene is complete!

In the opposing camp of diner devotees are the free-spirited subscribers to the diner ideal. The difference in their point of view is that no preconceived notions of origins or architecture cloud the diner experience. The group demographics: diner owners, truck drivers, grill men, busboys, waiters, waitresses, traveling salesmen, vacationers, and every other individual who loves bacon-lettuce-and-tomato sandwiches (anyone). This is the open-minded group that's willing to accept the possibility that using the word "diner" is acceptable, even if the building it refers to isn't a structure planned, prescribed, and prefabricated in a factory.

This second, sometimes stepchild category of diners is the unique breed of restaurants, cafes, greasy spoons, truck stops, coffee shops, drive-ins, hash houses, cafeterias, hot dog shops, and other out-of-the-way dinettes that follow the same operational rules of the classic diners, yet don't acquiesce to the strict architectural criteria as those operating in the "undiluted" diner form. Although not housed inside a diner-like structure, they use as many of the favored elements as possible. At their fundamental core they are diners, like it or not.

Like the real thing, these comfort food facsimiles occupy the unwanted hole-in-the-wall locations found in urban areas. Vacant lots, parcels of land near shopping areas, or the wide open space found alongside any road or highway are common locations. The one glaring difference is that they make practical use of whatever type of commercial structure is available. Along a downtown Main Street in Anytown, USA, one could easily find a diner taking the place once used by a retail shop. Further from the city limits, a diner might occupy an abandoned dance hall, a vintage gas station, and maybe even a barn. If those ephemeral qualities that make a diner a diner are present, any type of building will suffice.

Thrown in with this unholy category are the so-called homemade diners, utilitarian buildings constructed to appear as if they are factory-built, but crafted with more pluck and determination than those made of assembly-line components. Creative spin-offs in this realm of eatery include those diners constructed out of vintage trolley cars, abandoned rail cars, school buses, or even trailers! In this ad hoc classification of diner design, sheer imagination makes up for any lack of pedigree.

In the end, it's plausible that the common denominator of both the pure and the relaxed genus of diners is the visual clues such as the counter, stools, and booths. But adding those elements to the restaurant mix and stating that you were in the possession of a diner would be highly presumptuous. The basic truth is that the American diner is more than just a business where one plops down on a stool and orders food. No quantity of artificial ambiance, architecture, or decorative minutia is going to improve inferior food quality, lousy service, or dirty surroundings. What's more, an eatery that originates in a factory won't foster camaraderie, friendly atmosphere, or sense of community that both types enjoy.

Let it be written that a diner is an eatery that encompasses more than just the external and internal trappings of the physical sphere. A more realistic axiom would state that the people themselves make up the real essence of the "diner experience," for a diner is more than just a building style or interior motif. The true-blue, all-American, deluxe diner exists as a self-contained, ever-evolving microcosm of society and the community it serves.

CHAPTER ONE

BIRTH OF THE AMERICAN LUNCHWAGON

Portable Diners Conquer the Streets

"Once upon a time, many years ago, when there were ever so many kings and America was one of England's colonies, the hospitality of the road was extended by the friendly Inns which dotted the roadside. All over Europe and in many parts of America, lumbering stage coaches would pull up out of the weather before an Inn where the badly mauled passengers could freshen up a bit, rest, and, most important of all, eat. The Inn began to die with the advent of the auto. People could travel long distances and everybody got in a rush about going places fast and often. Where they used to look forward to stopping at an Inn, they began to count the number of Inns they could pass. Speed was everything. Sure the Inns are mainly gone now. But in their place is the hospitable Diner, offering relaxation and good food to the tired truck jockey, the traveling man, and to all who frequent the highways of America."

The Diner, Volume III, Number 6, 1946

The American diner was an idea born in the streets. The product of necessity and utility, its first incarnation came to life in the simple form of the pushcart and roaming food seller. The era was the 1870s, a time when the streets were cobblestone and fast-food restaurants were as far-fetched an idea as flying a rocket ship to the moon. In those days, corner convenience stores, gas stations stocked with snack foods, full-service coffee shops, and other roadside restaurants that kept their doors open 24 hours a day were the stuff that dreams were made of.

Imagine yourself lumbering down a rough cobblestone street in a horse-drawn wagon without a radio or heat. You're hungry, famished, have only a few pieces of change in your pocket, and the only businesses that serve food have closed for the night.

Even if they were open, dining there would be out of the question since the working man's salary you earn might only allow you to purchase a tankard of drink or small cut of buttered bread. Besides, with your clothes soiled from a day's hard labor (in the local mill or the factory), sitting down to dine at a fine city hotel would be a little embarrassing. What would you do and where would you go for an affordable, nutritious bite to eat?

As did the majority of city workers who toiled during the days of America's Industrial Revolution, it was more than likely that you'd grab a quick lunch from a walking food seller or pushcart vendor. These were lone wolf merchants, intrepid salesmen of the streets who—despite the fact that they had no shops of their own—still managed to reap an income from the passing clientele. It was a business of opportunity, one where being at the right place at the right time (with the right products) meant the difference between success and failure.

Suited for the go-getter, the job of street sales didn't call for a lot of training and it was easy to break into the business. Most vendors possessed a simple, two-wheeled wooden cart or a hand-held basket—anything that could hold a small supply of goods for sale. Unencumbered

ANOTHER QUICK LUNCH

Around 1907, the Quick Lunch Dining Car offered its bill of fare both "day and night" to the citizens of Rochester, New York. In terms of the architecture, this wasn't your typical lunch cart, proof that even in the early days, restaurateurs were calling other types of service buildings dining cars. *Preziosi Postcards*

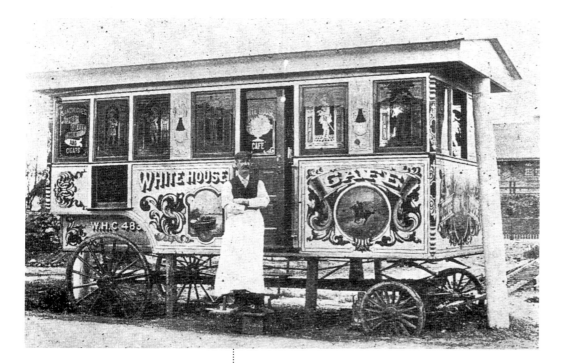

was free to roll or carry his portable storefront to any street or square.

For advertising, the only requirement was a loud, boisterous voice that could proclaim the delectable qualities of one's foods. From the back streets and alleys of the big city slums, city folk regularly heard the pleas of the young girls hawking their steaming wares to passersby: "Get your nice hot corn, hot corn, smoking hot, smoking hot, just from the pot!"

At the same time, Vienna sausage dealers cried exhortations for their own customers, entreating all of the passing pedestrians and those commuters riding high in horse-drawn carriages to "come and get your hot sausages!" Somewhere around the corner and up the block the roving tamale men issued their own call for customers, "Tamales, all hot, all hot, all hot!"

Long before the turn of the century and the proliferation of the American automobile, anything and everything that the arms could carry was fair game for the street merchant. The only prerequisites were that the items had to be relatively inexpensive to purchase, resistant to spoilage, and easy to resell.

As a direct consequence, all manner of hand-held comestibles were available, including fresh fruits such as bananas, apples, and pears. Simple

H. G. HEATHER'S WAGON

H. G. Heather owned and operated this utilitarian White House Cafe lunch wagon. During the later years of the 1800s and even into the 1900s, the fancy scrollwork and decorative embellishments that were painted on almost every portable dining wagon were in tune with the graphic motifs of the age. This wagon did business on Union Street in Atteboro, Massachusetts. *Preziosi Postcards*

by today's strangling health ordinances, governmental licensing, and sanitation laws, the field was wide open for the small-time street restaurateur with big ideas. He ruled the public corridors and

HAVEN BROTHERS DINER

This Haven Brothers modern-day night owl was recently spotted in the streets of Providence, Rhode Island, selling food to late-night customers. (The diner is a vintage Barriere Lunch Wagon, only the wheels are modern.) Sometimes things never change. In the business of diners, that's a good thing—especially if you love lobster rolls, beef stew, and strong coffee. *Jonathan Yonan ©1999*

A HORSE-DRAWN LUNCH WAGON
The Owl Night Lunch Wagon is currently on display at the Henry Ford Museum and Greenfield Village, Dearborn, Michigan. It's one of the last remaining original, horse-drawn lunch carts in the country and is a graphic example of how the restaurant business has changed. Before the start of the 1900s, "fast food" wasn't defined by the speed of service, but by the swiftness of your horse! *From the Collection of the Henry Ford Museum and Greenfield Village*

THE SCENIC LUNCH
Lunch wagon operators of the early days remained true to the simple names that evoked serenity and taste. "Scenic Lunch" conjured up images of the countryside for city-bound industrial workers forging a new America. This eatery appears to be part of a front yard business at the streetside. *Preziosi Postcards*

fare like salted popcorn and peanuts were favorite sellers, as were a variety of drinks. To wash down all of the "fast food" of the horse-drawn age, strollers could often obtain a small flagon of mineral water and, during the later years, a bottle of pleasantly flavored soda pop.

There were even vendors who specialized in dessert: during the summer heat, some roving Italian ice sellers did a brisk business serving flavored ice shavings on a scrap of paper for a single penny. In the financial district of New York City, Delatour's famous soda stand did an equally bracing business by selling chilled soda water enhanced by a rainbow of flavors.

Into this climate strode forth the "father" of the American diner, Walter Scott. At 11 years of age, young Scott hit the streets of Providence, Rhode Island, with his own basket full of goodies in a respectable attempt to ease his family's financial situation. If he could make an extra pocketful of change for himself at the same time, all the better.

Laden with fresh fruit, an assortment of hard candy, and a modest stack of newspapers, Scott became a regular fixture on the city streets. Walking the gas-lit avenues during the wee hours of the morning and serving all class of street denizen with his late-night snacks, Scott had ample time to ponder just what kind of business he had gotten himself into. There was no denying that this was an occupation that served insomniacs, ill-mannered municipal workers, and characters of dubious repute.

Even so, Scott took to the street vendor format like nobody's business and lifted the lowly sales occupation to a new height. When the American Civil War broke out, he showed his honorable qualities by volunteering for duty but didn't pass muster

PALMER'S STAR

Wagon maker C. H. Palmer advertised his lunch wagons (the Star is shown) to a fledgling industry with intricate drawings of his product line. The maker of "Fancy Night Cafes and Lunch Wagons," Palmer was based in Worcester, Massachusetts. *Preziosi Postcards*

WE SERVE THINGS GOOD AND HOT

During the early 1900s, generic postcards like this early example were used by lunch car operators to get the word out. Individual dining outfits could buy these cards in bulk, stamp their name in the appropriate place, and mail them out. *Preziosi Postcards*

because of his inferior eyesight. His vision handicap wasn't an issue for folks at the *Providence Journal*, and he was hired on at the publication to work double duty as a pressman and a type compositor.

As his contemporaries marched off to fight in the war, Scott continued building his roving night lunch business. By the time the war was over, he had carved out quite a reputation for himself with co-workers and other city employees. As workers at the *Providence Herald*, *Star*, and *Journal* strode in and out of their buildings between editions, there was Scotty, ready, willing, and able to offer them something good to eat at a fair price.

Fortunately (for the future of diners), the newspaper business held little opportunity for advancement. Prepared to strike out on his own, Scott abandoned his pressman post in 1872 and retired permanently from the newspaper business. He made a pact with himself, decrying that he would earn his daily wages by making, and then selling, food in the public market, the streets.

"I decided that I'd quit other work altogether," he revealed to a *Providence Journal* reporter some

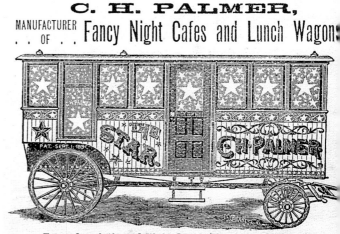

C. H. PALMER, MANUFACTURER .. OF .. Fancy Night Cafes and Lunch Wagons

Every description of Night Lunch Wagons made to order.
Correspondence Solicited.
OFFICE, 51 SALEM ST., WORCESTER, MASS.

decades later. "I figured I could build a good trade in a little while and make a decent living out of it." As it turned out, unforeseen circumstances put the lofty statement to the test: Twelve months later, the United States experienced a financial panic caused by land speculation and an over-expansion of the railroads. Scott burned all his bridges, and now he really had to give it his all.

Fortunately, the great "Panic of 1873" had no detrimental effect on Scott's plans. How could he fail? City dwellers were always salivating for a late night lunch and the existing foot-powered vendors offered only limited menus. Failure wasn't a part of the equation anyway, as in his mind he had already perfected a money-making scheme that was a stroke of street vendor genius.

The first part of the plan was to throw away the old hand-carried basket and use part of the money that he'd saved up

over the years to purchase a small, horse-drawn freight wagon. The second half of the strategy was to pick up an able draft horse. Definitely a unique arrangement, Scott's horse-powered vending outfit emerged from the workshop as a rather curious sight, indeed. He modified the wooden delivery wagon and added a makeshift cover to shield him from the elements.

For the most part, it looked like most every other delivery van of the day. The sides exhibited the biggest difference: One rectangular aperture punctuated each wall of the rig. Scott hacked them out himself, figuring that he could stock the wagon's cramped interior with prepared foods and

hand the victuals directly through these openings to the customers. And that's precisely what he did. From what were most likely the first "walk-up windows" in America, Scott solicited food orders from customers walking and driving along the carriageway, served it up, and collected the payment. Between the crush of daily feedings, he afforded himself the luxury of a small wooden box to recline upon (there wasn't much room inside for creature comforts).

Now, instead of wearing out the soles of his shoes and breaking his back by hauling around a heavy basket of food all night, Scott could conserve his energy and contribute more effort to improving

PERRIN'S CAFE

Situated in Altoona, Pennsylvania, Perrin's Cafe was yet another portable, horse-drawn lunch wagon that lost its mobility. In this particular case, the owners left one set of wheels visible. Note the opulent leaded glass windows. *Preziosi Postcards*

J. W. WICKSON'S PLACE

Space was tight on the inside of Wickson's White House Cafe. A good part of the interior was taken up by the massive coffee urn, the heating stove, and other kitchen equipment. Note the roll of wrapping paper on the left of the counter: These were the days before both paper and plastic. Customers carried away their purchase in their two hands. *Preziosi Postcards*

the food quality, the selection, and the service (establishing three important business fundamentals that would guarantee success to modern diner owners in the decades to come).

As an added convenience, a useful array of utensils, heating equipment, and extras that were once too big to tote became a regular part of his business. With this ability to carry a larger supply of food also came a bigger base of customers and increased profit. The best feature of the setup was obvious, since Scott could now pick up at a moment's notice and relocate the whole kit and caboodle! If sales began to wane along Westminster Street (one of Scott's favorite spots), he could hitch

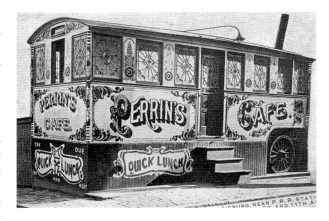

up Patient Dick (his horse) and move his wagon to more promising digs.

With that portability in mind, Scott wasted no time trying to capture the attention of the late-night audience and pulled up his "night lunch wagon" right in front of the *Providence Daily Journal* offices. During the 1880s, the city of Providence hummed with activity and hosted as many as three daily papers. Whenever a major story broke, one or more of the tabloids printed extra editions to inform the local readers of the latest happenings.

Of course, a heated competition arose that forced all three of the city publications to remain

on press for most of the day and night. This proved to be a boon for the enterprising Scott since after eight o'clock at night, the majority of local dining houses closed their kitchens until the next day. The only practical, affordable choice for the late-night city worker (who often didn't take the time to bring his own dinner) was to partake of the lunch wagon's specialized bill of fare.

After some initial reluctance, late-night workers, drunken carousers, insomniacs, street urchins, indigents, nighthawks, and a colorful assortment of felonious characters smiled upon the decidedly free-spirited lunch wagon and became passionate—if not loyal—customers. Urbanites appreciated the convenience of Scott's lunch wagon and rightly so: Whenever the mood struck them or the circumstance dictated, they could dine on hand-held foods like sandwiches, boiled eggs, baked pies, and hot coffee.

No domestic kitchen of the day—or housewife for that matter—was as flexible when it came to the satisfaction of hunger pangs and the slaking of thirst at night. Just like the little lady at home, Scott prepared from scratch. Because his Spartan lunch wagon didn't have the room to house a miniature kitchen, he cooked at home all the food he sold. Then he packed it inside the wagon and pulled it

by horse to the street customers. In terms of preparation, it was substantial work.

For this reason it was best to keep things simple. Using a limited list of edible ingredients, lunch wagon cooks owed it to their customers to get creative with basic foodstuffs and make them appealing. Above all else, a lunch wagon man had to innovate. This unspoken creed led to one of Scott's most famous and well-liked inventions, an entree he christened the "chewed sandwich." A distant cousin of today's shredded sandwiches made of brisket, this streetwise tidbit was born of opportunity and thrift, consisting of nothing more than scraps of meat and bread.

The recipe was simple: First, he collected fragments of meat from the cutting board and chopped them up into a fine mash. Next, Scott slathered some home-baked bread with a generous dollop of mustard or butter and placed the lump of minced meat in between the two slices. Viola: here was a lunch wagon special—a tasty, yet inexpensive sandwich customers could sink their teeth into.

With satisfying, yet affordable items such as this, Scott's lunch wagon gained a solid reputation for taste and price. Five cents was all that a luncher needed to pick out a meal, and for that price he could choose from a modest list of choices.

Regular items included the always popular ham sandwich, a boiled egg-and-buttered bread combo, or a single piece of pie for dessert (this was

SCOTTY'S PIONEER LUNCH

Walter Scott is recognized as the father of the American diner. He began his career in 1872 with a hand-carried basket and then simplified his streetside vending business with the aid of a pushcart. Later, he modified a horse-drawn delivery wagon to serve food and set the business of diners into motion. His specially built "Pioneer Lunch" wagon was once a popular eatery in the city of Providence, Rhode Island. *Gabriele Witzel ©1999*

NO-WHEEL WHITE HOUSE

As more and more cities decreed that the lunch wagon was a hindrance to normal street traffic, diner operators headed for vacant lots and available real-estate. Before specialized wagons could be built, entrepreneurs simply boarded over the wheel cutouts and fixed their unit to the ground. *Preziosi Postcards*

COLUMBIAN LUNCH

The Columbian Lunch added a retractable awning to the front of its lunch wagon to shield customers from the hot summer sun (it sold ice cream). Decades later, canvas or metal awnings would still be used at the American diner. *Preziosi Postcards*

THE PALACE DINER

After diners were forced to remain in one location, they took up residence in urban centers, wherever they could. During the 1970s, brick and other coverings were used to hide their real identity, as was done with this Middletown, Connecticut, diner. *Pedar Ness ©1999*

a great food value since a "slice" of pie in those days was about half a pie). For the well-off businessman (called the "dude trade" by wagon owners) choosing to slum it among the unwashed street rabble, Scott offered a plate of sliced chicken for the princely sum of 30 cents.

As would be expected during times of monetary depression, there were many a penniless customer who gobbled down a late-night dinner and then refused to pay for it. To discourage a procession of tramps from engaging in this ghastly practice, Scott perfected the crazy habit of reaching out of one of the serving windows to snatch off the deadbeat customer's hat. Before the ne'er-do-well had time to disappear into the darkness without paying, Scott took possession of the man's derby, fez, or top hat.

Diner folklore suggests that Mr. Scott could even "sense" when customers planned to stiff him with the bill. If he got that feeling in his gut that foretold of an impending rip-off, he'd make a preemptive grab for the offender's hat and then hold

on to it tightly. Sometimes, there were more than two dozen bowlers (and other styles of head covering) piled up in a corner of the lunch wagon, all waiting for their owners to return with the cash. In that rare instance when Scott was too slow to seize a man's hat, he trounced him on the head with a billy club! It was an effective deterrent, to say the least, and "Get a hat, or give a sore head" became Scott's signature slogan and claim to fame.

As Scott continued to secure his legend via this unorthodox customer service, a mob of competing outfits rose up from the cobblestone. One of the most memorable of these fledgling lunch outfits was run by a local man named Ruel Jones, a former Providence police officer who often observed the frenetic pace of the night lunch business during his overnight patrols (and most likely, he handcuffed and arrested a few of the rowdy customers who got into heated rows with the pugilistic Scott).

Jones became disillusioned with the risky nature of his work and decided that selling quick

food at the curbside was a much healthier occupation than chasing down armed criminals. According to historian Richard Gutman, author of *The American Diner: Then and Now*, Jones got started in the business when he contracted local wagon-builder Frank Dracont to build him a custom lunch wagon in 1883. This was a major milestone in the history of what would one day be called a "diner," as Jones designed his wagon just for selling food. It was the very first unit designed specifically to operate as a lunch-vending wagon.

By the mid-1880s, the art of selling convenience food in the street was growing up to become a genuine, respectable business. New lunch wagons had to reflect an upgraded image, both in terms of their design and decoration. To his credit, Jones' inaugural lunch cart surpassed the visual and functional aspects of Scott's first effort: The wheeled compartment featured a splash of red paint and sported a serving counter on one side, foreshadowing an important element that eventually became a diner standard.

Jones' new rig also possessed a few additional refinements, the most notable being the Jones family name prominently displayed on the windows. The entire wagon setup was an unabashed attention-getter, a rolling advertisement built for attracting customers and satisfying the call of late-night hunger.

As Gutman tells the tale, Jones' business boomed, and by the year 1887 he managed to establish a respectable chain of seven lunch wagons. All were quite successful in plying the late-night fast-food trade in the streets of Providence. Every morning, city dwellers heard the evidence of this successful operation as Jones' long caravan of horse-drawn lunch wagons clip-clopped back to the Jones house, where workers restocked cabinets with

NEW YORK STREET VENDORS

By the turn of the century, street vendors became a permanent fixture of the American city scene. Competition was fierce, so hot dog and snack food vendors like these New York pushcart merchants (circa 1906) often expanded their serving business by purchasing a small lunch wagon. Before long, the streets were clogged. *Library of Congress/Detroit Publishing Company*

PIG STAND NUMBER 18

During the early teens and 1920s, diners were gaining a foothold in New England. Meanwhile, curious little stands known as "drive-ins" were making great inroads in areas where climate permitted automobile owners to dine in their vehicles year-round. In a few short decades, this open-air format would spell trouble for most diners. *Courtesy of Richard Hailey/Texas Pig Stands Inc.*

provisions and watered the horses. If ever there was a successful chain food operation, this was probably the earliest known example.

Inspired by the daily wagon train, competitors who had desires to build their own fortune in the street-side food serving business popped up like so many hot biscuits. By October 1884, Ruel Jones' cousin Samuel Messer Jones, at the time an out-of-work mechanical engineer, decided that he would also join in the expanding parade of lunch wagons. Impressed by the buzz of the night lunch business in Providence, Samuel Jones borrowed a couple of hundred bucks from a friend to get started. He took the easiest route and followed Walter Scott's basic example. Once he found a cheap express wagon of his own he purchased it and hastily converted it into a working lunch rig.

Samuel Jones knew there were many operators milking the Providence market, so he decided to buck convention and roll out the first lunch wagon of its kind in Worcester, Massachusetts, a respectable distance away. There, he claimed the corner of Main and Front streets as exclusive sales territory and with that, began to build the town's respectable diner legacy serving one egg sandwich at a time.

Despite the uninspired format of this first eatery, Samuel Jones didn't lock himself into the same old lunch wagon mentality. As a trained designer, he held a distinct advantage over those who were merely salesmen. He was thinking of new ideas constantly, trying to improve the current state of the art. Once on his feet, he came up with a new lunch wagon twist of his very own, adding a distinct option that made it physically comfortable for customers—or "diners," as restaurateurs later called them—to make themselves at home and eat.

Although it took him a few years of working in the streets, by 1887 he scratched together the $800 of capital (that's a lot of egg sandwiches) he needed to turn his fanciful insight into reality: His

PROVIDENCE LUNCH WAGONS

This aerial view of the Crawford Street Bridge in Providence, Rhode Island, depicts what life was like during the late 1890s. Horsepower was used for all modes of transportation, as well as the pulling of wagon-wheeled lunch wagons. During those times, competing food vendors thought nothing of pulling up their wagon to an existing seller and taking advantage of a good location.

LLOYD'S DINER EXTERIOR

In the category of roadside food, Lloyd's diner is an oldie but a goodie. It was built back in 1940 by the Worcester Lunch Car company. The original owner was Richard Whitney, an old-time diner man who operated the eatery on the corner of Route 122 and Route 280 in the town of Orange, Massachusetts (where it remained from 1940 until 1990). Richard Lloyd purchased the building, restored it to its original condition, and moved it to a new location on Fountain Street in Framingham, Massachusetts. *Coolstock ©1999*

AN ABANDONED DINER

Today, finding a worn out, vintage classic like this abandoned dining car is becoming more and more of a rarity. Avid collectors and dedicated diner restorers are snapping up all of the available units and bringing them back to life. *Jonathan Yonan ©1999*

THE ALL NIGHT LUNCH WAGON

In Providence, Rhode Island, Hoyle Square was often the site of the All Night Lunch Wagon. These were the early days of the diner, a time when making profits meant moving from location to location, depending on the amount of pedestrian and carriage traffic. Apparently, some sort of public works project was underway at this intersection, providing a ready market for food. *All rights reserved, the Rhode Island Historical Society*

dream was an improved, expanded serving wagon that featured enough room inside for the patrons to stand. With that sort of lunch wagon, neither rain, sleet, snow, wind, or the chill of a winter's night would deter the customers of the street-side vendor from chowing down on their favorite food.

Samuel Jones' first "distinctive night lunch wagon," as he called it, wowed the festival-goers who attended Worcester's New England Fair. The electrifying response was appropriate, since his fully engineered prototype was more than a lunch wagon jerry-rigged from a junked horse-drawn carriage. This wagon provided a real taste of the future and hinted at improved diner designs to come.

Inside, the Jones lunch wagon came equipped with a complete kitchen, just like the kind that house-builders installed in the most modern homes of the age. The only difference was that Jones miniaturized his on-board galley with the

hopes of conserving weight and space. The end result was a bounty of leftover floor space inside, leaving plenty of square footage for that all-important asset known as customer standing room.

Prospective buyers witnessed firsthand that the Jones wagon was unconventional both in layout and looks. As evidenced by the finish and trim, it was obvious that this model was definitely a cut above the rest—much more than just a weather-tight place to wait for food. In the interior, all of the woodwork reflected the skills of a master carpenter. Decked out in finest timber and polished finish, it exuded a sense of luxury. There were no rough boards, rotted timbers, or peeling paint evident in this wagon.

Also quite fetching in the Jones design were the decorative windows. For today's diner historians, graphic etchings culled from advertisements of the age reveal the detailed work of the master glazier. Here was a style of stained glass panels that transcended mere windows and propelled the ordinary diner toward a new aesthetic. But this treatment wasn't only a matter of excessive decoration. Artfully etched among decorative flourishes were five words that described the standard menu of the late-night lunch wagon: sandwiches, coffee, cake, pie, and milk.

Not surprisingly, this embellishment quickly became a standard of all lunch wagon designs. When Jones' competitors in Worcester and other New England cities rolled out their own lunch boxes on

wheels, they also incorporated this sophisticated format of listing the standard foods. With such beauty and grace casting its shadow on the ordinary, there was no more room for do-it-yourself treatments and hand-painted signs. Elegant and refined, the lunch wagon was now an eclectic form of portable architecture.

Rightly proud, Jones took his new wagon around the city and set up shop at the busier spots, securing an enormous following. Before long, he had built up an exclusive clientele and, in some people's opinion, a closed monopoly on the quick lunch.

continued on page 26

STREET CAR DINER

Marie's Street Car Diner is one of the few classic homemade diner survivors, located in the heart of the old stockyards area of Fort Worth (Cowtown), Texas. Photo circa 1986. *Coolstock* ©1999

THE CUTCHOGUE

THE CUTCHOGUE DINER
Main Road, Cutchogue ★ Long Island, New York

It was Olin Glover who first introduced comfort food to Cutchogue, New York. In 1933, he built the town's first wooden diner on a plot of land on Main. The business later became so successful that he bought a brand new, stainless steel-and-porcelain enamel dining car and had it installed on site. After the Kullman Dining Car Company delivered the train-like structure, he converted the old place into a storage room and connected it to the rear of the new structure. The sparkling diner became the jewel of Main Street.

Glover sold the roadside beauty to Al Harker in 1948, and it was renamed Al's Diner. Locals remember Big Al for his grillside manner and great food. In those days, the cooking was done in the front, where customers could watch. What stuck in people's memory was the fact that Harker often performed his cooking tasks with a cigarette dangling out of his mouth, playing very much the part of the stereotypical cook. But in spite of his smoking, he cared about taste and quality, and often went out to catch fresh bluefish when in season. He packed in the crowds with his good food and defined the diner's golden years.

In 1965, Harker sold the place and passed on the dream to the new owner, Bill Hagen,

who picked up where Harker left off and ran the diner until 1981, when Diane Slavonik and Jennie Kapustka (a pair of former waitresses) took their stab at the business. They renamed the classic Kullman the North Fork Diner and ran it only until 1985. To the surprise of some locals, David De Friest came on board next. He also ran the local funeral home.

Two years later, the quaint little diner on Main Street was once again for sale. When John Touhey spied the ad in the classifieds, he worried that someone might buy the gem and not appreciate it for what it was. Making his living as a low-income housing developer in New York, he owned a summer house in Cutchogue and figured that he could buy the diner, preserve it, and make a go of the restaurant business. "I was buying the beauty of the diner, the potential of the building itself," he recalls. "I didn't put a lot of thought into running a restaurant because I was still naive about it."

Despite his inexperience, Touhey purchased De Friest's diner and took it back to its roots, renaming it the Cutchogue.

While he toiled to perfect the consistency and taste of the menu, he completed all of the

CUTCHOGUE DINER EXTERIOR
The Cutchogue Diner is a 1930s-vintage Kullman. On this same plot of Main Street land, Olin Glover built the town's first wooden diner in 1933. The small eatery became so successful that he bought the stainless steel-and-porcelain enamel dining car (shown here) and had it installed on site. *Ronald Saari*

omelets to choose from, just old-fashioned combinations of eggs, bacon, and pancakes. The dying creed of quality and freshness guide the cooking. When a customer orders a turkey sandwich, it's a real bird roasted in the oven—not a tasteless, processed hunk.

The same protocol of simplicity is followed with the dinner menu. For the traditionalist, there's real pot roast, complete with gravy, mashed potatoes, and a vegetable—all for $7! Customers can choose from a variety of meat dishes, fresh fish, and nightly specials that range from spaghetti to leg of lamb. The desserts are a dream, and manager Cathy Dickson makes them from scratch. Baking three times a week, one of her specialties is a peach pizza, a pie with homemade crust, peaches, and crumb nut topping. The selection of after-dinner treats is the one area where the menu diverges from the ordinary. As a result, some of the customers come in regularly—just for the desserts.

restorative work over three years, as he could afford it. The kitchen required all-new fixtures, as everything in there was junk. "I don't know how they were operating the place," Touhey said.

A thorough cleaning inside and out uncovered a lot of great stuff, too. When Touhey first bought the diner, the ceiling looked like it was made from brown-colored tile. When he got up on a ladder to take a closer look, the true nature of the ceiling was revealed. A swipe of the finger proved that it was enameled tile all right, only the real color was white with tiny specks for accent. A proper cleaning brought the overhead surface back to life.

There were more surprises revealed: When the dark-stained paneling on the front wall was removed, a surface of beautiful cream-colored tile work was uncovered (a nice complement to the interior, since the other colors were maroon and silver). But nothing could prepare the new owner for the gift he received when he pulled off the cork board covering the wall above the counter, where previous owners tacked up daily specials. There was yet another cream-colored wall, emblazoned with two maroon hallmarks.

Touhey liked the look of these art deco–inspired logos so much that he duplicated the design throughout the diner. The streamlined signature became the official logo for the Cutchogue and was soon found above the entry door awning and on all the menus and stationery.

By this time, the interior was completely restored to the glory of its early days. To match the new decor, the food was finally up to snuff too. These days, it's basic, down-to-earth fare at the Cutchogue. At breakfast (the busiest meal) there are no fancy

During the winter months, the clientele is made up of locals and everybody knows everybody. There's the after-church Sunday crowd, the laborers who stop by for lunch, and the dedicated regulars who come to sup each day. Two retired men come in for all their meals, taking their usual stools at the counter. Another octogenarian gent stops by to visit four or five times a day. During the summer season (from April to October), the place gets hectic. With so many nearby vineyards and beaches to visit, families stream in from New York to rent houses. Since more and more people are tired of fast food, the Cutchogue is packed full, and customers must wait outside the front door.

Aware of the timeless appeal of quality and service (and the growing nostalgia for diners), Touhey has no intention of ever selling his Main Street gem and plans to keep it going "as long as possible." If the landlord decides that he wants to use the property for other reasons, he plans to pick up the Kullman and relocate it elsewhere. "I view myself as someone who wants to preserve the diner the way it was and improve it," he says with conviction. "My aim is to preserve this art piece and make it a better restaurant."

DUTCH DINER POSTCARD

Located on Route 22 in Shartlesville, Pennsylvania, the Dutch Diner was the typical barrel-roofed model of the 1920s with a new twist: The roof was extended upward to resemble the silhouette of any barn found in the Pennsylvania Dutch region. For diners, anything to attract attention was good. *Courtesy of Roger Jackson*

continued from page 22

While Jones worked the city streets, Charles H. Palmer (known by local residents as the "Worcester wit") took close notice of the popular lunch operation. Palmer witnessed that everyday at six o'clock, Jones pulled up stakes and called it quits for the day. This presented a unique timing opportunity that was just waiting for someone to exploit.

According to *The Diner* magazine, Palmer got the idea to work this "after six" shift and decided to pick up where Mr. Jones left off. His reasoning was sound, as there "were a lot of people going to the theater, to square dances and sewing bees, drinking in the saloons, and so on . . . who had to go home sometime."

Eventually, these after-hour revelers would want something to eat or drink. Palmer's hunch proved to be correct and his new night lunch operation did exceedingly well. By the time Mr.

Dutch Diner
Located at Shartlesville, Pa.
on famous Rt. U. S. 22

Jones was ready to streamline his own growing business and sell all his lunch cars except one, Palmer had earned enough money to buy them and take over the business they pulled in.

Jones may have been an engineer, but Palmer was a visionary. He saw even more potential in the format and by September 1891 had the foresight necessary to take out America's first patent for a lunch wagon. As difficult as it was to believe, no one had even bothered to do so up until that time. Nevertheless, the design specs outlined were far from original. Like so many other lunch wagon makers, Palmer defined his unit with a rectangular, 6x16-foot, enclosed body. Made from a wooden frame and shell, he set his dining box on a wheeled

THE WHITE MANNA

Hackensack, New Jersey, is well-known in diner circles for the White Manna Diner. Equipped in very much the same way as the early lunch wagons, the White Manna remains an uncomplicated favorite for Garden State residents. *Ronald Saari ©1999*

PTOMAINE TOMMY'S MATCHBOOK

Ptomaine Tommy's was a Los Angeles restaurant (circa 1942) that got its start as a roving lunch wagon (circa 1913). Poking fun at the dubious quality of food that served at a minority of the early wagons, Tommy's capitalized on the frequent occurrences of "ptomaine poisoning" and made it part of its image. This was the "Home of the Original Size." *Preziosi Postcards*

OKLAHOMA BOOM TOWN DINERS

Located in St. Louis, Oklahoma, these workaday diners, or cafes, were at one time the center of a bustling Main Street in an oil boom town. Farm Security Administration photographer Russell Lee documented this moody scene in 1939. At both restaurants, "Sandwiches," "Hot Lunches," "Plate Lunches," or "Short Orders" were available for a modest price. *Library of Congress*

undercarriage. The stern of this shack extended out over the front wheels.

At the rear, it was just the opposite: This end had contoured cutouts to accommodate the high, large-circumference wheels that operators relied on to ford the muddy streets and rutted avenues of the day. Beneath these wagon wheel cutouts was imprinted the bold inscription "Pat'd Sept. 1, 1891." A small step ladder arrangement fastened

extreme. It was difficult to see through the window panes, as every inch of the glass had ornamental etchings of decorative fluff (including the serving windows and those in the door). Every portal had a large star smack dab at the center, surrounded by a swirling, dizzying constellation of smaller ones.

Palmer called this celestial version "The Star," complete with his own name and additional decorative work painted prominently on both sides. Customers accepted the motif with little reservation, as

THE PALACE CAFE
During the early years of the 1900s, the diminutive Palace Cafe (a former lunch wagon) was a busy vending stand located in the growing town of Rahway, New Jersey. The business prospered and after the installation of a modern, prefabricated dining car, evolved to become the Palace Diner. *Preziosi Postcards*

below the doorway aided ingress and egress to the serving and preparation compartment. For all intents and purposes, it looked like an eccentric circus wagon where—instead of wild animals—humans came to feast and drink.

An elaborate window treatment upped the ante on the earlier Jones version and pushed the commercial art of lunch wagon decoration to the

vaudeville houses, dance halls, hotels, and other grand monuments of the age incorporated many such baroque themes into their own design. When inscribed upon glass, these busy patterns of filigree, elaborate crests, and intricate scrollwork became the neon lights of the pre-electric age.

Palmer called the cheaper, economy version of this dining vestibule the "Night Lunch Wagon."

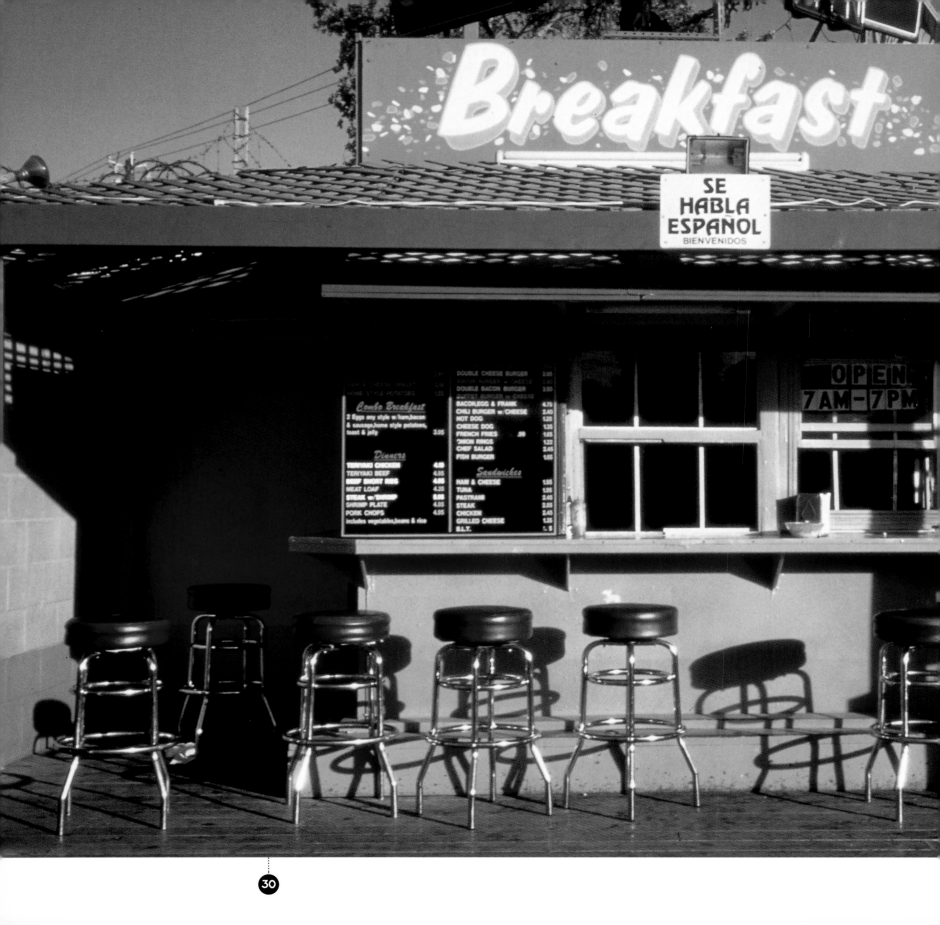

SANDWICHES

GRILLED CHEESE	140
GRILLED HAM AND CHEESE	250
HAMBURGER	175
CHEESEBURGER	195
TUNA SALAD	225
STEAK	275
HAM	225
PASTRAMI	250
HOT DOG	150

NO 5 CORNED BEEF HASH 475
POACHED EGGS

BLUE MOON SPECIAL

3 EGG OMLETTE 425

HAM SAUSAGE CHEESE ONION
PEPPERS BROCCOLI MUSHROOM
ABOVE ANY 3 ITEMS PER OMLETT

Like its more expensive sibling, it came predecorated as "The Owl," an appropriate name that eventually became the default title for late-night diners. Compared to the premium "Fancy Night Cafe" and its engraved windows, it was rather drab and sported only one etched glass panel in the door. The decorative styling on the exterior wood exhibited a more reserved demeanor, with a minimal use of inscriptions. Moving horizontally around the two-tone body, a modest strip of painted filigree added a somewhat graceful touch.

As historic diner advertising shows, these models were merely the beginning when it came to the many types of lunch wagons that Palmer manufactured. When customers called for customization, only the amount of money one was willing to spend limited the design. Palmer built food wagons to please, and he promised to deliver "lunch wagons of every description made to order."

Oddly enough—despite all of his manufacturing flexibility and the many innovations that Palmer contributed to the field—he never came to dominate the early trade of American lunch wagons. During those formative diner days, a raft

DINER MENU BOARD

From chalkboard to hand-painted sign to the changeable letter board, the diner menu display has changed drastically over the years. In the good old days, it was good enough just to scrawl a few specials on a piece of cardboard—today, only neon and eye-popping images will attract a diner's gaze. *Jonathan Yonan ©1999*

LOS ANGELES DINER STAND

Diners do business in many forms. Whether it be a coffee shop, city cafe, or roadside stand like this California shop, eateries were in the pink as long as they offered the type of edible goods that the public desired. *ChromoSohm ©1999/Unicorn Stock Photos*

EARLY DAYS OF THE MAYFAIR

The Mayfair Diner began life in 1928 as the Morrison and Struhm Diner in Philadelphia, Pennsylvania. In 1932, it was moved north to a growing part of town called Mayfair. As business grew, it was joined by a larger O'Mahony and was then supplanted by a completely custom-built, incredibly long (188 1/2 feet) O'Mahony during the late 1950s. Today, the Mulholland family continues to operate the restaurant, serving huge crowds of customers the same homemade food that made all of this diner success possible. *Courtesy of Debbie Mulholland*

of competitors were all jockeying for position. The one person who possessed the right combination of luck, panache, and know-how would rule the kingdom.

As industry magazines and popular history tell the tale, it was a former janitor by name of Thomas H. Buckley who managed to cook his way to the top of the vending heap. Within a few short years, he rose from relative obscurity in the urban restaurant trade to become the reigning royalty of the industry. He was the man hailed far and wide as the "Original Lunch Wagon King."

A former lunch wagon counter boy and also the owner of an Owl wagon himself, Buckley literally gained entry into the business through the kitchen door. As told by Richard Gutman, he whipped up quite an impressive oyster stew and had great plans

to secure his fame and fortune by serving the delicious dinner to the public (oysters became a passion for American diners as early as the mid-1820s). But—as often happens with dreams and schemes— fate forced another course. It didn't take long for Buckley to figure out that he had to shuck lots of oysters to strike it rich and, consequently, his plans didn't really pan out. He deemed that building the wagons that actually served up the food at the street-side was a far more lucrative alternative.

He dubbed his first notable line of wheeled eateries "the White House Cafes," a procession of lunch wagons that mimicked the Palmer models in basic design and decoration, save a few aesthetic variations. He continued working to refine his line of products and in 1891 unveiled a brand new wagon he christened the "Palace Cafe." A year later,

ARRIVAL OF THE MISS ADAMS

Joe Wilusz owned the Miss Adams diner when it was first delivered to this site in Adams, Massachusetts, in late 1949. It didn't have far to travel, as this was a Worcester Lunch Car, Number 821. Today, the Miss Adams is under the stewardship of Barry and Nancy Garton, proud owners who continue to run it in the same traditions of the old days. *Courtesy of Barry and Nancy Garton*

Harbor Diner — Lake Shore Drive — Phone 2550 — Dunkirk, N. Y.

70108

THE HARBOR DINER POSTCARD

"Cleanliness—and Good Coffee!" What more could one ask of their neighborhood diner? Located on Lake Shore Drive in Dunkirk, New York, it appears that the Harbor Diner started out as a single unit that was added on to more than once. During the 1930s and 1940s, regional food specialties like fish dinners ruled the diner menu, and it wasn't unusual to see individual mom-and-pop operators (like Ma Gierner) promote their own family name instead of a national company or brand. *Preziosi Postcards*

he organized a concern called the New England Night Lunch Wagon Company and set upon the task of turning out portable food parlors in ever larger numbers.

Although it took more than four weeks to build one of his units, Buckley's Grafton Street manufacturing facility in Worcester was capable of rolling out as many as eight lunch wagons per month. He established his business by 1893 and gained notoriety with one of his own designs. That year, the patent office granted Buckley his first patent for a lunch wagon, a variation that he founded on the placement of windows all around the car—the front, back, and sides. Patrons liked all of the portals, as they made the cramped space inside the tiny lunch car seem a lot less confining.

As the name implied, the White House Cafes were pristine and strove to pull the industry further away from its working-class, beanery image. Following the current fashions, Buckley's cafes featured windows made of frosted glass as well as panes of blue-and-red flash glass. Using patriotic hues proved an effective way to gain attention and also provided a pleasant form of illumination inside the car. He enhanced this theme of nationalism by etching the portraits of Washington, Lincoln, Grant, and other famous presidents directly onto the window panes (for some reason, Ulysses S. Grant was the most popular request for lunch wagon window panes).

Historical photographs provide a clear glimpse of the Buckley style: On the outside of the wagon, he favored a base paint job of bright titanium, providing an expansive canvas that just begged for additional decoration. To conjure up those pleasant, familiar images that men liked, he commissioned artists to paint elaborate hunting scenes, lush landscapes, and other pictures of supposed historical importance (famous battles, historical figures, and so on) on all four sides of the rig. Surrounding these intricate cameos was a heavy arrangement of blue-and-gold scrolling, accompanied by heavy block letters that formed the words *The White House Cafe.*

As *The Diner* magazine editors of the 1940s reported, Buckley came up with many great features and "changed the width of the car from six feet to ten to give the customer comfort and the operator ease of operation." As the writer elaborated, his innovations didn't stop there as, "He was the first manufacturer to think of customer and operator as a combination."

He equipped his cars like no other lunch wagon, with stools that were more comfortable than the standard models and a coffee urn that gleamed of bright nickel. Designed specifically to "impress customers and to give the operator lasting wear," it was elaborate. Not only that, the serving counter inside was quite substantial, boasting an expanded width. During times of inclement weather—when inside space was at a premium—customers were bold enough to lean on it and eat their food there!

But there was more to come. In 1892, Buckley took the lunch wagon form to the final level when he created a version christened the "Tile Wagon." Intended as a promotional model to tour of exhibitions and state fairs, the Tile Wagon took more than a year to construct. With features such as German plate-glass beveled mirrors inlaid with lace work tracery and carriage lamps hand-crafted of hammered silver, one could easily see why it cost more than $5,000 to build the rig. Hands down, it was the most expensive wagon to date.

Curiously enough, the expense was well worth it. Buckley gained more free publicity from the wagon than he could ever afford and took the idea of the diner to new markets. As he showed

MURRAY'S WHITE DINER
In the diner town of Worcester, Massachusetts, Murray's Diner relied on the coffee-drinking customer during the late 1970s. Of course, having an illuminated Pepsi sign high above pulled in some of the younger crowd. Although simple in design, the double-barrel roof gave Murray's a unique attitude. Sadly, this little neighborhood joint is no longer with us. *Pedar Ness ©1999*

YANKEE DINER INTERIOR

The Yankee Diner on Route 20 in Charlton, Massachusetts, keeps the interior arrangement simple, just like it was when this diner first rolled off the assembly line. Note the old-style, covered stools and the porcelain-clad panels under the serving counter. The only thing missing is a counter man with white shirt, bow tie, and spatula in hand. *Pedar Ness ©1999*

the public just how fantastic his creation was, he garnered 140 different prizes in showings across America. By far, this was the best that the American diner industry had to offer and no other lunch car company could hope to upstage this rolling ambassador.

Inside, the Tile Wagon was a gilded marvel of particular opulence. Here, every surface—including the floor, walls, and ceiling—shone like ethereal stone with glistening opal tiles! To provide lighting after dark, intricate statuettes made of gold and ivory held glass oil lamps high in the air. Even the stools featured polished nickel platforms with glass coverings! An ornamental cash register made out of polished brass competed for attention with gleaming spittoons, decorative edging, and other polished metal. Ordinary homes were not this nice.

And so, with Thomas Buckley's debut of the grandiose Tile Wagon, the portable roadside restaurant known as the lunch wagon achieved its maximum state of expression. This was an important milestone in the nation's diner history, as it signaled the final step in the evolution of the animal-powered, high-wheel, wagon-style of streetside vending apparatus.

Without question, horse-drawn vehicles had reached their design limits. Further improvements would change the rolling food van into something completely different. More important, the gasoline-powered machine known as the motorcar would soon take over the streets of the city and, as a byproduct, would bring with it a more frenzied way of life. Against this backdrop of speedy travel, increased mobility, and diminishing space, the late-night, quick lunch eatery would adapt.

To survive in this strange new environment, the lunch wagon had to evolve into a new format that offered customers more convenience, spaciousness, and social interaction. The decorative embellishments that did nothing but further the visual aspects of the dining experience would no longer be sufficient to attract customers. Merely pouring a pot of money into building a better wagon wasn't enough. More useful arrangements that augmented the consumption of food and drink would take precedence.

Speed, economy, quality—and of course, customer service—would become the watchwords for the unfolding diner industry as diner designers and restaurateurs began the move toward a more utilitarian dining format. Without a doubt, function would soon take authority over form. The full-fledged American diner—a 24-hour, dedicated restaurant operation that had no wheels, remained static, and held a position permanently along the roadside—was an institution that would soon be in great demand.

The next stop in roadside dining was just around the bend. Its time had come, as the once-hectic era of the roaming food vendor and the roving late-night lunch wagon was drawing slowly to a close.

DINER NEON SCULPTURE

Jerry Berta creates diner sculpture like this glowing example at his diner studio in Rockford, Illinois. Using ceramics and neon, he manages to capture the pure spirit of the early diners and mold it into a mesmerizing piece of art. *Jerry Berta ©1999*

CHAPTER TWO

FROM HOT DOG WAGON TO DINER

Perfecting the Roadside Food Parlor

"And the one thing that is as American as Honest Abe has never come into its own, plays no part in our wistful remembrance of things American. I refer to the lunch wagon. In all the restaurant businesses throughout this nation there is no other form so predominantly American as the Dining Car. Even the name 'Lunch Wagon' reeks American terminology. The features of its service are American—speed, simplicity, sanitation; its appearance is definitely solid American; even the stools in which we sit are American in principle; in brief, it is as American as turkey. But there is no unity, no pleasant thought that there is something national, something that belongs to this country alone. It is only the foreign writers who visit this country who recognize the fact. We ignore it. And yet the Dining Car could be built up into something that would be just as much a national institution as Congress itself. What are we going to do about it?"

The Diner, Volume I, Number One, 1940

As dining wagons began to take up permanent residence in the streets, they encountered fierce competition from established restaurants. While the small-town operator had a lock on the late-night market, the story was altogether different in major metropolitan areas. In large cities such as New York and Boston profiteering saloons took the rivalry to the brink by pairing the age-old pastime of drinking with an appropriate companion: eating.

This practice of offering imbibers a stomach full of food—at so-called bargain basement prices—was nothing new. According to historians, barkeepers began the habit of doling out a "free lunch" long before famous diner pioneer Walter Scott was born.

It all started around 1837 at the St. Louis Hotel in New Orleans, Louisiana. One day, a barman named Alvarez was serving a group of businessmen from the French Quarter when a complaint arose about the food prices. Fed up with what they thought was an unfair arrangement, the merchants squawked about paying restaurant rates for the meager lunches they wolfed down. Where was value?

As a gesture of goodwill, the barkeeper decided to try something new: All of the noon hour customers who bought and paid for a drink received access to a free lunch. The local men loved the idea and soon the place was brimming over with a crowd of daytime drinkers eager to down a brew and fill up on the food. It proved to be a profitable promotional idea, since the average customer drank a lot more spirits than the value of what he could ever eat!

Not to be left out, other hotels and bars copied the practice and within a few short years, the early form of the "buffet lunch" spread to drinking houses all over the land. If Clancy laid out a better spread than Dinty did, he got all the business. Before too long, men viewed the American lunch hour as a convenient excuse to hit the bars and down some spirits. By the turn of the century, ordering a 15-cent glass of wine gave one access to a table full of food in many of the better drinking establishments!

YANKEE DINER INSIDE
The residents of Quechee, Vermont, know where to go when they want to sit at the counter and experience some authentic diner fare: the Yankee Diner. There's no Gorditas, Big Macs, or Blizzards sold here, just a simple menu of good old American food and drink made (and served) the way it used to be. *Ronald Saari ©1999*

MISS WORCESTER

The Miss Worcester diner is known by diner fans far and wide. It was constructed by the Worcester Lunch Car Company of Worcester, Massachusetts, and today resides at the "psychic center" of the American diner world. Why? It's right across the street from where the old Worcester factory used to be. Here is a real diner's diner, neat and tidy, quick with a tasty lunch or a refreshing drink, with a personality few eateries can match. Could this be where Ronald McDonald dines on his days off? Maybe not, but in the early days, this location was used as a showcase for the Worcester product line. *Pedar Ness ©1999*

THE OWL CAFE

The Owl Cafe depicted in this historical image might be the quintessential example of the converted trolley car. While this outfit looks rather clean and tidy, it wasn't always true with the worst of the converted transit vehicles. *Preziosi Postcards*

and go, as most workers had to make quick tracks back to the office or factory. It took no longer than 15 minutes to consume their noon meal (and at least a half-dozen drinks).

This was a relatively easy thing to do, since bar owners set up the complimentary spreads for speed and self-service—not for looks or dining etiquette. At most bars, they piled a long, unadorned counter with mounds of premade sandwiches, cold meats, and cakes. To get their free share, the men milled past the spread in a single line and thrust out hands to serve themselves.

For all the hungry and thirsty, the big city bars were a tremendous deal. But there was more to it than just filling your belly with cheap grub: During the Gay Nineties, many considered drinking to be an art form. And—as *The Diner* magazine reported years later—there were "a lot of men studying art." Much to the chagrin of their teetotaling wives, mothers, and sisters, many men lingered and often failed to return to work or home. Bars didn't have established closing times, so it wasn't uncommon for the weaker sex to remain in the saloons all night.

It was during these trying times for women that Charles Buckley and his lunch wagons came to the rescue. By no accident, he sold a substantial

It wasn't a pretty sight: Once matrons served the food, the rowdy customers tore into it with what one observer referred to as "inconceivable rapidity." The frenzied scene was one of gulp, gobble,

MIDWAY DINER SNOW

Captured on film in 1978, this frigid Midway diner scene evokes the calm and serenity one feels when they know there's a favorite place they can go to get a tasty bite to eat and meet friends. The Midway was a classic located on Route 20 in Massachusetts. Unpretentious mom-and-pop diners like these caused many to fall in love with the format. Today, the Midway is no more. It has been cut into two sections; one piece resides in Vermont, the other in somebody's back yard. *Pedar Ness ©1999*

FOG CITY INTERIOR

In San Francisco, California, the Fog City Diner serves an upscale menu to trendy customers. These days, it's become more than just a diner and has become a recognized and popular part of the city's nightlife. *Courtesy of Real Restaurants Inc./Fog City Diner*

number of his eateries to the Women's Christian Temperance Union in New York City. As an organization formed to rally against the evils of drink, the group was highly visible in trying to save the morals of the American man and would stop at nothing to achieve its goal. Within the confines of the lunch wagon, the women found their secret weapon: food.

Women knew by experience that one of the most effective ways to influence a man was through his stomach. To test their theory, they set up a number of the Buckley wagons in working districts where groups of men congregated. By 1898, they had eight of these rolling food outlets operating in New York City. There, men could obtain a tasty, economical meal that far exceeded the quality of the local bar lunch and most other competing lunch wagons.

The home-cooked menu was a definite bargain. To lure the men out of the watering holes, they set the prices ridiculously low—so low that the reform wagons barely made a profit. For one thin dime, a customer could pick up a cup of good hot coffee and a meat dish that came served with vegetables, rolls, and a small dessert. Profit or not an important principle was at stake here, and the women of the WCTU would stop at nothing until they saved men from the lure of alcohol and its evil influence.

As the temperance women refined the lunch wagon's image, their good deeds came back

around to bless Buckley's business. His operation prospered, and in towns across the country he could count 275 lunch carts operating as his very own brand. Riding high on the string of successes, he got the notion to open a large, permanent

GRAND ISLE NUMBER 13

Diner maker A. H. Closson built this distinctive-looking lunch wagon for diner man Art Dawson. Open for business in Whitehall, New York, this innovative lunch wagon was wired for electricity and featured running water (a built-in storage tank was installed above the driver's seat). But the innovation didn't end there: Both sets of wheels featured leaf springs to cushion the ride to and from the day's place of business. *Preziosi Postcards*

NONPAREIL DINER

Operating in Oaks Bluff on Martha's Vineyard, William V. Ripley was the proprietor of the Nonpareil Diner. He attested that his diner was "the World's most Sanitary and proud dispenser of Pure Food served by a body of Gentlemanly Clerks that are always looking after your Comfort and best interest to the extent that you get nothing but the very best." *Preziosi Postcards*

restaurant in Worcester, Massachusetts, but couldn't match the same success. Sadly, he lost more than $25,000, went bankrupt, and met his untimely death in 1903.

Despite these unfortunate developments, the T. H. Buckley Company remained a vibrant concern. Two years after its founder's death, the diner maker debuted a new wagon design with a well-designed floor plan. In this carefully executed model, the small kitchen area featured a clever, U-shaped serving counter. To add more dining space, a convenient eating "shelf" protruded along the inside perimeter. Stools ran along its entire length.

Although from the outside it looked similar to most of its forerunners, the most recognizable difference in this new Buckley model was the wheel arrangement. Instead of installing four of the high, wagon-style rims that allowed operators to quickly move from site to site in the dead of night, designers equipped it with much smaller-circumference rims. The entire dining box sat low to the ground and was a lot less forgiving of terrain.

This was an important step in the design of the urban dining unit, as cities began to strip

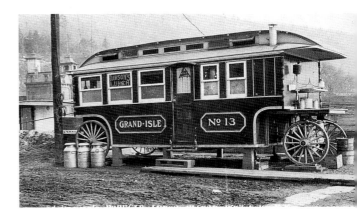

America's lunch wagons of their mobility. With motorcars claiming the streets, most city corridors became a maelstrom of activity. Amid the din of motorized vehicles, horse-drawn delivery vans, hansom cabs, carriages, bicycles, pedestrians, and trolley cars jockeyed for position. With so many lunch operators trying their hand at the business, there was little extra space or room to move around.

In the city of Providence—the recognized birthplace of the diner—disgruntled citizens began complaining about the overcrowded street conditions. It appeared that a flagrant abuse of the rules prevailed and many of the town's lunch wagon men were in blatant violation of their operating permits. Instead of packing it up and closing down at dawn, some of the vendors stayed over, working well into the morning hours. This caused no end of trouble for commuter traffic and other street-bound commerce.

Forced by public opinion to take notice, the city fathers instituted an immediate crackdown. Others followed and soon, up and down the Eastern seaboard, officials placed restrictions on all of the street vendors who worked out of moveable dining rigs. Some

municipalities banned food wagons from the city boulevards altogether, while others instructed the lucky ones to vacate the streets by 10 a.m. or be fined.

It was ironic that the handy portability afforded by wheels—one of the key qualities that made the mobile lunch wagon so successful—suddenly became a liability. (It's interesting to note that for many years thereafter, a number of the "planted" diners kept their wheels in place to escape the higher property tax rates that cities levied on the fixed eateries.)

To stay in business, the legions of lunch wagon operators had to take leave of the streets. Worse than that, they had to relinquish their portability and do business in one place, all the time. In the months that followed, a mad scramble for available territory ensued as the lunch wagon men withdrew from the busy streets and made their exodus to the four corners of the city.

Fortunately, many cities offered empty parcels of land and vacant lots that lunch wagon operators could buy or lease. A few unscrupulous sandwich men simply pulled their wagons onto someone else's land and worked the crowds until its owner used physical force to evict them. As luck would have it, basic lunch wagon design helped in all of these cases: Because early diners of this ilk were so compact, they could easily occupy second-rate nooks or crannies that wouldn't suit any sort of normal business. And with that, the stationary, permanent diner was born.

As the former mobile lunch wagons filled in the chinks of the American metropolis, many major cities initiated the switch from horse-drawn trolleys to electric-powered ones. In 1897, before the lunch wagons even had time to settle on foundations, the cities of Boston, New York, and Philadelphia replaced their horse-drawn cars with electric cars. Suddenly, there was a large surplus of trolleys that had no useful purpose other than scrap.

Of course, this presented a few go-getters of the age with a chance to make a fast buck. The idea was simple, albeit crass: Pick up a number of the used trolley cars at a bargain price (as some accounts record, for less than $20 apiece), throw in a coffee urn, a small griddle (with a vent pipe),

LLOYD'S OF LOWVILLE

There's Lloyd's of London and then there's Lloyd's of Lowville: One organization insures your valuables, the other ensures your appetite is satisfied. This photograph is vintage 1972, documented in Lowville, New York. Step on the gas and head upstate; Lloyd's is still slinging the hash. *Pedar Ness ©1999*

"A good place to eat"
MAPLE VIEW DINER
Maple View, N. Y.

MAPLE VIEW DINER POSTCARD

Before World War II, the American roadsides were defined by the individualist—the mom-and-pop operator. For the go-getter, it was easy to start up a business in those days. There was little red tape and environmental regulation. National corporate control of road and highway commerce had yet to exert its stranglehold. Like this setup in Maple View, New York, many families who owned a gas station and an adjoining diner actually worked there and lived in a house out back. *Courtesy of Brian Butko*

BING'S CONVERTED DINER

Bing's Diner was one of those great little diners made from a former trolley car (the headlamp is a dead giveaway as to the building's origin). Located in sunny Castroville, California, the artichoke capital of the United States, Bing's was in its prime during the late 1970s and served patrons breakfast, lunch, dinner, and what else—barbecue. *Pedar Ness ©1999*

a few plates, and some utensils, and you had yourself a cheap, working lunch car. Who needed the luxury of a costly Buckley?

In theory, it was an excellent idea. Trolleys of the day often boasted a handsome finish and bright colors. Some of them even came with interiors built of costly rare woods, others with lush Wilton carpets, window shades of Russian leather, and fittings of polished brass. In some cars, the interior lampshades were glass. At the time, the makers of trolleys believed that spending good money on a handsome-looking car was one of the best ways to attract passengers to ride the lines.

Unfortunately, these once-beautiful trolley cars became wilted flowers by the time the transit lines released them from service. When companies decommissioned commuter cars and renovators refitted them, continual use and vibration made them more of a candidate for the junk pile. Ready to fall apart, they were drafty during

the winter and not very efficient at keeping out heavy rain. Roaches hid in the many crevices and air poured through the many openings. As a warm, dry building that intended to house lunchers with a modicum of comfort, they were ill-suited.

Most of the time, the trolley lunch found its way into disreputable areas of town, or the "wrong side of the tracks" where rental rates were cheap and no one cared. It really didn't cost that much to get a trolley lunch going, and consequently, a substandard class of owner emerged. Attracting birds of the same feather, they became all-night hangouts for disreputable clientele and the criminal element. When they were out to round up the usual suspects, the cops always descended on the trolley lunch outfits to pick up the night's line-up. It didn't take long for the cities of Buffalo and Atlantic City to ban them.

To the wagon owner's intense dissatisfaction, the pundits painted many of the above-board beaneries with the same broad brush. After years of polishing up their image, diners became the butt of jokes vis-à-vis the trolley. Even worse than all the reputation problems, the widespread trolley use forged the first restaurant-to-train car connection. Because of the widespread proliferation of the trolley car-turned-eatery, many of the people who didn't grow up during the early days of the lunch wagon took up the fanciful notion that the late-night diner originated from the trolley. Like it or not, this association would dog the diner for years to come and continue to shape emerging architecture.

As the trolley lunch cemented its dubious

reputation, major cities in America began to experience a tremendous influx of daily commuters and shoppers. Lunch wagons were no longer the only alternative for the urban diner, and America's restaurant boom was on. In the two decades that followed 1910, the estimated number of eateries increased almost 40 percent.

It wasn't long before a diverse range of budget-minded coffee shops, lunch counters, cafeterias, taverns, and other eateries began to fill the streets with the familiar smells of bacon, eggs, and steaming coffee. By that time, more than 20,000 automobiles cruised the roadways in the United States and the diner industry prepared itself for a rapid expansion. The only thing that the restaurant owners and

manufacturers had to get a handle on was how to extract all that money from the passing cars.

Electrified by the burgeoning market and the potential to take it as their own, three major players emerged to corner the lucrative lunch field: Philip Duprey of Worcester, Massachusetts; P. J. Tierney of New Rochelle, New York; and Jerry O'Mahony of Bayonne, New Jersey. As a group, they formed the holy trinity of American diner makers and shaped the industry for decades to come.

Duprey was a successful insurance salesman and real-estate agent and had an eye for a sweet deal. He decided that making food wagons would put him in the black, so he started up a diner

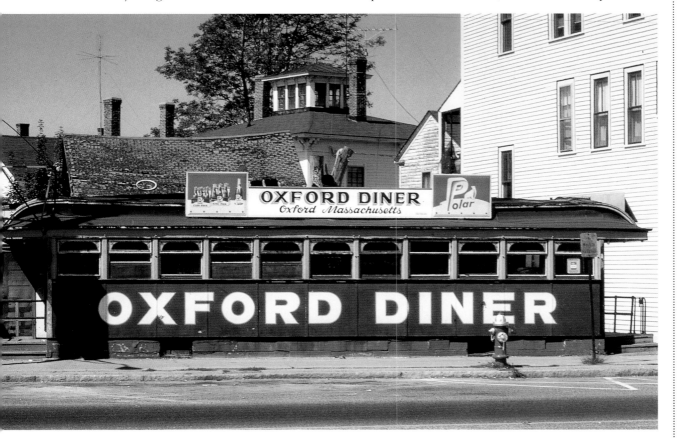

DOHERTY'S QUICK LUNCH

The ability to grab a "quick lunch" has always been a selling point for restaurants. It still is. Many of today's modern chains have offered their customers a free meal if lunch isn't delivered within a specified time frame. This speedy server was located in Lynn, Massachusetts. *Courtesy of Larry Cultrera*

manufacturing outfit and called it the Worcester Lunch Car and Carriage Manufacturing Company. To get his business up and running quickly, he bought out the entire stock and trade of another local lunch wagon man, Wilfred Barriere.

In 1907, Duprey's company rolled out its first lunch wagon (registered as serial number 200, for the sake of appearance) and called it the American Eagle Cafe. Similar to the ornate White House Cafés and stylized Buckley models, builders decorated the box in the same fanciful treatment that was so popular at the time. Even so, it broke new ground with a monitor roof that had a raised clerestory with operable window vents.

The graphic overkill seen in this first model eased by the time the company produced its ninth unit. By that time, Duprey subdued the tricky roof treatment and changed it into a more simple monitor style. The elaborate paintings on the exterior panels became subdued graphics as well.

On the inside, all of the booths and trim were crafted of wood. Duprey moved the kitchen from the side and squeezed it lengthwise. As an adjunct to this change, he equipped the unit with a long serving counter that ran down the middle of the box. Permanently attached to the floor, a row of low stools provided the seating. In years to come, this soon-to-be typical diner layout paired up with an even more innovative convenience: electricity (soon freezers, toasters, mixers, slicers, and a plethora of time-saving gadgets complemented the kitchen).

DORSEY'S DINER

In 1972, Dorsey's Diner was the place to go in Wallingford, Connecticut, for steaks, chops, and every other diner food one could think of. The place couldn't help but exude a homey feeling. Today, fine artists are taking painstaking efforts to recreate real-life diner scenes just like this one and reproduce them on canvas. Today, we need more places like Dorsey's and fewer places with intercoms and back-lit menus. Unfortunately, this baby burned down a few years ago. *Pedar Ness ©1999*

Historical records reveal that the company built 651 diners in all and added a glorious new chapter to the Worcester legacy started by Samuel Jones so many decades ago. Evoking a certain sense of quality with understated elegance, the Worcester lunch wagons were very well-received among the diner men. Over the next 50 years, the company's basic design saw few changes, if any.

P. J. Tierney, also in the American diner dynasty troika, got his start in 1895. He learned the many tricks of the lunch wagon trade by operating his own outfit, working long, hard hours until he had enough cash to buy a second wagon. He continued to roll over the profits into the business and, by 1905, managed to build up a small chain of 38 units. Having climbed that craggy peak, he cast his eye on the construction end of the business.

With boundless dreams, the first chapter of an American success story began: From a small garage located in New Rochelle, New York, Tierney cobbled together what he thought a modern lunch wagon should be. Dipping into his well of hands-on experience, he designed and built an attractive and functional eatery. As fellow dreamers proved the practicality of the motorcar in cross-country races, he began selling his lunch cars for $1,000 apiece.

With the large quantities of lunch cars he rolled out, Tierney could afford to be a little generous. As explained in *The American Diner: Then and Now*, he sometimes took one-fourth of the total payment down and allowed a buyer to pay the rest of the money on time. Every once in a while, he even took in an old lunch wagon as down payment. On rare occasions, he handed over one of

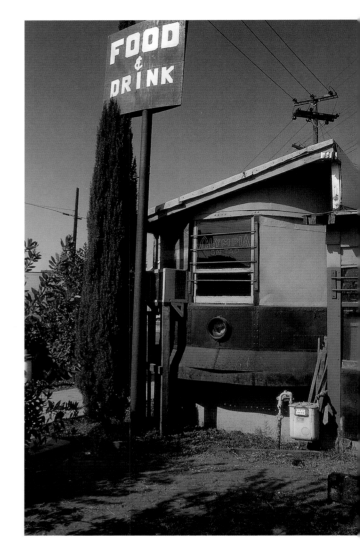

his lunch units simply on the promise to pay. Endowed with flexible business terms and a far superior product, he became a millionaire by the time he died in 1917.

The restaurant industry remembered Tierney for many of his achievements. Who could forget? He was the visionary who eliminated the outhouse and brought the toilet inside. He was the first to install a dining car at a permanent location (according to the sales literature distributed by the company). He equipped his lunch cars with tile, installed skylights, exhaust fans, ventilators, and replaced kerosene lamps with electrical lights.

Tierney's sons inherited all of these innovations as their foundation and proceeded to build a strong industry upon them. They had one or two business ideas of their own and in 1923 spun off the Tierney

OWL DINER SIGN

Charles Palmer manufactured a lunch wagon that he called "The Owl" during the early 1890s. It was such an appropriate moniker that many diner men used the name for their businesses—even though their lunch wagons were not made by Palmer's company. This fantastic neon sign is part of the Owl Lunch (a vintage Worcester Lunch Car) located in Lowell, Massachusetts. *Jonathan Yonan ©1999*

Operating Company as a separate entity. The company offered public stock and set a lofty goal: It would open one new company-owned diner every week and continue to do so over the next four years. It wouldn't rest until 200 Tierney diners lined the highways and byways.

At the same time, the company stepped up production rates in its factory and expanded facilities. By the mid-1920s, the Tierney brothers were building a diner day! It was a big accomplishment for the time, and they weren't

imponderables as how to wash dishes, the correct way to prepare foods, and the proper method for ordering supplies.

If one took into account the customer service of the Tierney Company and the timeless quality of the Worcester builders, it would appear that there was no room left for any other diner maker. For a few years, that was true—at least, until that fateful day Irishman Jerry O'Mahony came upon the

FOOD AND DRINK
Historically, diners and train cars have always been linked in one way or another. Could it be that the long, windowed shell of a former railroad car makes a handy diner building? This retired Fresno Traction Dragon Car was pressed into service as a depot to get "Food and Drink" in Fresno, California. *Glen Icanberry ©1999*

shy about it. Right on the side of the factory were painted the words, *The largest manufacturer of dining cars in the world!*

With all those impressive numbers, one might think that selling diners and sending the buyers off to fend for themselves was the only thing the Tierney brothers saw any interest in. They weren't. The company was a real stickler when it came to operator competency. As an insurance policy against early failure, they formed their own specialized training school. During the two weeks that it took to build a customer's car, the future owners attended the company's lunch wagon college. There, they learned the many tricks of the diner trade. The informative curriculum covered such

scene. Here was a man who absolutely loved the dining car field and one who didn't feel satisfaction until he improved the core elements of the industry.

O'Mahony got his first taste of the restaurant business while working at his father's bar and grill in Bayonne, New Jersey, and many believed that he had diners in his blood. Around 1910, he threw in his lot with his brother and the pair bought their first dining car, located in the Big Apple (as luck had it, it happened to be a Tierney-built model). The eatery was a big hit and before long they expanded from owning one diner to owning eight.

MURPHY'S CAFE INTERIOR
Murphy's Cafe was the second American Eagle Cafe to be built by the Worcester Lunch Car Manufacturing Company. Note the fancy lighting fixtures and the elaborate, etched windows. During the late 1900s, the standard diner elements were beginning to emerge, despite all the ornamentation, and included a large coffee urn, serving and diner counters, and stools for customers to sit on. These were three very important elements. *Courtesy of the E. B. Luce Corporation*

THE PENN DINER

On West 33rd Street in New York City, the Penn Diner operated opposite Penn Station as a full-service motoring station during the 1920s and 1930s. "A Good Place to Eat," city dwellers with automobiles could get Socony Mobilgas there as well as a quick bite. As city real estate values rose, many such locations would become a rarity. *Sol Libsohn, from the series* Food for New York City, *1939.*

MISS BELLOWS FALLS

Located in Bellows Falls, Vermont, the Miss Bellows Falls is on the National Register of Historic Places. It's a Worcester Lunch Car Company model, complete with barrel roof, eight stools, and five oak booths. In continuous operation since 1942, it's a true diner survivor, one that will be here to thrill diner lovers (and road warriors) well into the next century. *Pedar Ness ©1999*

That modest chain of eateries was only the beginning. In 1913, O'Mahony teamed up with a new partner, John Hanf. The duo took close note of the dining structures the competition was building and made plans to improve them. With nothing but pluck and determination, they embarked on a plan to build their own wagons. To their satisfaction, they sold their first for $1,900.

As the gasoline-powered automobile replaced the horse-drawn carriage, the pair cranked out model after model, refining their design as they went along. In the beginning, all of their new iterations borrowed elements from the previous motifs. O'Mahony dining cars clung to the barrel-style roof and adopted much of the exterior pageantry exhibited by the early wagons.

It was there that the design philosophy diverged. While O'Mahony models were no thicker than 10 feet deep, they stretched out to 26 feet across. The offset door typical of the early Owl lunch moved to the center of the box, and five fancy windows flanked each side (making a total of ten). Despite all the etched glass and decorative lettering painted on the sides, the early O'Mahonys provided a clear picture of the budget eatery's future. In the decades to come, diner builders (in almost every instance) arranged the struc-

ture as a symmetrical rectangle. The diner was a long boxcar equipped with an inside serving counter that divided the customer ordering/dining area from the kitchen.

One thought-provoking article published in a postwar issue of *The Diner* cited that all of the dining car manufacturers that came before O'Mahony were content to build practical, workmanlike cars. Dining in these utilitarian places, the public "knew what to expect: good food and low prices." The prevailing attitude of some short-sighted people working in the lunch car industry was that "If they wanted anything else, let 'em go to the Waldorf!"

It's a good thing that Jerry O'Mahony refused to accept this attitude. As the article explained, he reasoned that "a man ate a whole lot more and enjoyed it better in pleasant surroundings." In later years, it was this philosophy that led him to
continued on page 54

BOOTH SERVICE MISS BELLOWS FALLS BOOTH SERVICE

1950s DINER JUKEBOX

Part of the counter arrangement at Moe's Diner in Cleveland, Ohio, this curvy, 1950s-era jukebox head is recognized by both young and old alike. It's a magic box, a countertop entertainer that plays the memories of yesteryear and speaks loudly of a time that many regard as "the good old days." *Ronald Saari ©1999*

WIMPY'S PHOENIX DINER

Wimpy's Diner was in its heyday during the 1950s and 1960s and did a great business at its location on Seventh Street and Indian School Road in Phoenix, Arizona. The owners, Paul and Marjorie Roberson, knew just what the customers liked and gave it to them. The story behind the name? Wimpy gained notoriety as the cartoon character of Popeye fame who was often heard saying, "I'll gladly pay you Tuesday for a hamburger today!" *Courtesy of Mike Roberson*

Pal's Diner

PAL'S DINER
6503 28th Street SE ★ Grand Rapids, Michigan

On a cold winter's day in 1993, a small gathering of folks assembled inside Pal's Diner. Above the clinking of coffee cups and the sizzle of hamburgers, one could hear the steady drone of voices. But few were laughing that day.

For all the regular patrons (who already consumed their own weight in Pal's coffee), this was to be the last cup of Joe in their beloved diner. Pal's, a local icon since 1954, was scheduled for permanent closure. The next day, February 4, a Rockland Electric Company worker would arrive to throw the final switch. The juices that gave Pal's life would be cut off.

In the meantime, customers reminisced about Pal's legacy, the early days when John DeZurney purchased the diner from the Manno Dining Car Company in Belleville, New Jersey. He installed the pink enameled-and-stainless steel diner on Route 17 South, just north of the Ramapo Avenue overpass in Mahwah. There, it became a permanent fixture for 39 years. Christening the diner "Pal's" was appropriate since DeZurney greeted patrons with "Hi Pal, what'll you have?" With John's congenial attitude and home cooking, customers came to view Pal's as home.

Pal's was the favorite haunt where starry-eyed lovers pledged their unswerving devotion to each other. It was the sanctuary of road-weary truck drivers—a place to get a good hot meal and a warm smile. It was also the "in" spot where friends could meet after a late night on the town. And, it loosed the kitchen shackles of many a housewife, providing a deserved break from cooking and doing the dishes.

Pal's was also the scene of at least one dramatic and dangerous scene. It happened in 1959 when a woman burst in screaming for help. Her husband was chasing her across Route 17 with a gun! Thinking fast, employees hid her in the food locker. Out in the lot, the man looked around, yelled obscenities, and fired the gun. The bullet shot right through a glass panel at the front of the diner! Shaken but safe, the woman thanked her rescuers, left the diner, and was never heard from again.

After that, day-to-day activities remained routine until 1974, when DeZurney sold the diner to George Vardoulakis. To everyone's satisfaction, the Pal's name remained, and customers barely noticed the change. The new owner believed in the same sort of hospitality.

That's something that beautician Annie LoPolito found out—albeit the hard way—in 1985. She had sold her business and was in the process of moving to sunny Florida with her new husband, when the pair stopped at Pal's. While she was using the rest room, her husband took off, taking all of her money and possessions with him. She was stranded with only 17 bucks to her

PAL'S ROUTE 46 LOCATION

Pal's Diner began its life in the town of Mahwah, New Jersey, on the highway designated as Route 46. During the 1950s and 1960s, it was a roadside fixture and taken for granted by many, until that fateful day when it closed for business permanently. Barry Brown purchased the diner, trucked it to Michigan, and reopened it under the same name. Who says diners go out of business? Many just move out of town. *Preziosi Postcards*

PAL'S DINER AT NIGHT, EXTERIOR
Built by the Manno Dining Car Company, Pal's Diner incorporates many of the popular postwar design elements. Not only is most of the exterior sheathed in stainless steel, but neon tubing is incorporated as an important facet of the construction. With the restaurant competition heating up after World War II, the diner manufacturers did all they could to instill the American diner with a sense of style and excitement. *Courtesy of Barry Brown*

the little diner was doomed. Fortunately, Barry Brown managed to work a deal in the 11th hour with Robinson Cartage, a Michigan trucking firm that was up to the challenge.

By February 4, everything fell into place. That day, the Browns and David Scripps, president of Robinson Cartage, met in front of the New Jersey landmark to see Pal's off. Also on hand to bid a fond farewell to the local hangout were Vardoulakis, LoPolito, and many loyal patrons.

name and no place to sleep. True to form, Vardoulakis offered the abandoned woman a waitress job and a group of truckers donated money for an apartment.

The good favor was not forgotten. As a Pal's waitress, LoPolito extended customers her own brand of friendship in the form of a warm greeting and a welcoming smile. She became a permanent fixture and liked it so much that she worked there until the day it closed. Vardoulakis often joked to customers, "Annie goes with the diner."

In June 1992, the land lease for Pal's expired and that's when the trouble began. To everyone's amazement, the new landlord raised the rent from $700 to $7,000 a month. Vardoulakis was forced to put Pal's on the market. When a Michigan couple, Barry Brown and Sam Choi Brown, heard of the diner's fate, they flew to Jersey to look Pal's over. The diner won their hearts and they immediately began negotiations to buy it.

While the couple worked out a deal, a local historical group started a campaign to block the sale. When the land owner found out, he informed Vardoulakis of his intent to demolish the diner. With Annie LoPolito's help, the Browns initiated a wave of faxes, phone calls, and letters in an effort to speed up the negotiations. According to Barry Brown, "Annie was the glue that kept the deal together."

There were more concerns: How would they move the diner after the sale? Unlike some diners, Pal's didn't split apart for easy transport. Eight trucking firms turned down the moving job, and it appeared to everyone that

One heartbroken man leaned up against a telephone pole and began to cry. With tears in her eyes, another woman pleaded with Barry Brown to take the loose brick from the front steps and use it at the new site. For years, she told her husband to "watch out for that brick." Some took final snapshots and others gathered into small groups as a hush fell over the parking lot. With careful respect, workers gently hoisted Pal's up onto the transport trailer.

During Pal's final parade, a police escort accompanied it through New Jersey, Pennsylvania, New York, Ohio, and Michigan. The trip concluded on February 11, 1993, when the Manno diner completed the final leg of its journey of I-96. For the next two years, Pal's occupied a storage lot near the Kent County Airport. During that time, Barry Brown, his father, and a friend worked to restore the diner to its original condition.

Pal's reopened in April 1995 and made its new home at the Cascade East Shopping Center in Kentwood, Michigan. The cozy diner once again calls out to all those seeking a good meal and a place to relax. Up on the roof, glowing bands of neon and a classic diner clock beckon to the passersby. Inside, a pink, backlit ceiling, boomerang Formica, Naugahyde stools, booths, an authentic 1954 jukebox, and a vintage Woolworth's soda fountain work in unison to take customers back. As the breathtaking Manno known as Pal's makes new memories, long-time customers back in New Jersey are smiling—a tear in the eye.

HARLEY DINER

The Harley Diner is part of S. E. Harley-Davidson in Cleveland, Ohio. After all, diners aren't just for those who arrive in automobiles. Be it a plane, train, skateboard, or motorcycle, commuters of all kinds appreciate the unaffected atmosphere of the American diner. *Ronald Saari ©1999*

PTOMAINE TOMMY'S JOINT

Ptomaine Tommy's was a Los Angeles restaurant (circa 1942) that got its start as a roving lunch wagon (circa 1913). Poking fun at the dubious quality of food served at a minority of the early wagons, Tommy's capitalized on the frequent occurrences of "ptomaine poisoning" and made it part of its image. This was the "Home of the Original Size." *Preziosi Postcards*

continued from page 50

begin the era of stylized cars. Never mind that the O'Mahony style evolved into a format that took its cue from the railroad car. With their brick-like figure and monitor deck roof, his diners gave purveyors of the hamburger sandwich a new level of lunch wagon beauty.

By the early 1920s, O'Mahony cars completely shed the outdated format of the roving street vendor. With their modern construction, it was impossible to mistake them for old, outmoded lunch wagons. They were bigger, longer than they ever were, hugged the ground, and commanded attention. Most noticeable was the fact that they had a lot more windows to look out of.

As it happened, factory-built restaurants began to look more and more like train cars. Because of the close resemblance, one author (who was writing an article about the O'Mahony company) suggested that the name "dining car" be used when referring to them. Eventually, street slang distilled the formal title, and later it resurfaced as "diner." Leave it to Jerry O'Mahony to make the moniker a part of restaurant culture: In 1924, he splashed the word all over a company sales catalog and unofficially, the eatery for everyman had its permanent name.

Around the same time, diner companies began to introduce a myriad of improvements. While wood still comprised the framework of the Worcester cars, the company upgraded the exterior of their products by attaching colorful panels of porcelain enameled steel (this was a boon when it

AGAIN ENLARGED A LITTLE TO SERVE YOU BETTER

JEROME DINER

Most likely a Tierney brand diner of the 1920s, the Jerome Diner plied its trade in the Richmond Hill area of Queens, New York (on 101 Jerome Avenue). For the Roaring Twenties, this place was the best that diners had to offer. By this time, the lunch wagon was all but gone and Prohibition was in full swing. *Preziosi Postcards*

came to resisting the elements). Some diner makers, such as Brill and O'Mahony, took durability a step further when they began building with steel.

With the added strength and rigidity, it became possible to construct even larger, more elaborate diners. This ushered in all sorts of additions, as the stronger floor beams and walls could now withstand more load. Ceramic tiles appeared as the standard diner flooring and even migrated up onto the back walls. Long serving and dining

counters made of heavy marble ran the entire length of the diner, as did an endless row of cast-iron stools. Throw in a few large coffee urns, a stove, hamburger griddle, and insulated cooler, and you had enough weight to buckle even the most durable wooden diner.

As the length and girth of diners expanded, a variety of new equipment filled the space. The tiny stoves once found in the Jones and Buckley wagons were now a cruel joke. Real restaurants that came equipped with all of the normal, "life-sized" cooking gear, diners included griddles, steam tables, ice boxes (in later years, refrigerators and freezers), and sandwich boards. Storage cabinets took control of any leftover space. To the delight of customers, the battered tin cups and wax paper of the street era were replaced with attractive dishes, glassware, and respectable table settings. Diner owners with any real sense knew that the presentation of food meant a lot to the customer.

For seating, stools ruled the 1920s, and the back bar area behind the counter was off-limits to the customers. This space was the sole dominion of the cook and counterman, a character of American lore who doubled as waiter, dishwasher, and busboy.

In the cramped, linear space, he learned how to conserve his movements, shuffle from side-to-side, attend to one station and then another, and finally, return gracefully to serve the customer. Over time, seasoned operators became proficient at what some diner veterans refer to as the "counterman shuffle." To make it easier to move around (and to keep from slipping on grease), some of the best hoofers even seeded the floor with sawdust.

For the most part, diner men had to be pretty light on their feet, as it took a respectable chunk of change to maintain a successful eatery. You had to sling a lot of hash to pay off a note, make the utility payments, and cover the food bill. More often than not, it was operator speed and service that

BOULEVARD DINER

In Worcester, Massachusetts, the glowing neon of the Boulevard Diner lights up the night. For those with a fondness for diners and vintage road-side architecture, it's a warm, welcome glow that draws them near. Food, friends, and an escape from the hassles of modern-day living await them inside. *Jonathan Yonan ©1999*

pulled in the extra income in the form of tips and gratuities.

Even so, diners weren't out of the question for working-class dreamers who wanted to open their own business. After World War I, anyone could get into the business. You didn't need a degree or extensive training, as long as you had the $7,000 to $9,500 it took to buy a fully equipped Tierney Car, or the $4,500 to $7,500 required to secure a Worcester rig (or the credit to buy on time).

Yes, the year 1924 was a great time to purchase a diner: eager to attract returning servicemen who were itching to start their very own grill, the big three diner makers did all they could to perpetuate the postwar building boom. At the time, the model proffered by Tierney was perhaps the best value on the block. For one turnkey price, the company

DINER INTERIOR POSTCARD

Pennsylvania's Willow Grove Diner was a place that boasted a classic diner interior, complete with a service counter, stools, booths, coffee urns, jukebox selectors, hat racks, tiled flooring, neon lamps, menu boards, venetian blinds, cooking area, waitresses, and more. Along with the happy customers, these are the elements that made the American diner famous. *Preziosi Postcards*

THE FORMOSA CAFE

The Formosa is a restaurant made from a converted train car located in West Hollywood, California. Here is an excellent example of the mismatch that occurs when trying to make one thing into something it isn't. Ill-suited to handle modern conveniences, the train car roof of the Formosa takes on a rather unattractive appearance with that addition of air-conditioning and other modern environmental machinery. *Pedar Ness ©1999*

supplied diner buyers with the structure and everything needed to get started. This included the proverbial kitchen sink, pots, pans, stove—even a cash register.

With deals like this, the American diner industry saw a rapid expansion over the next three years. A raft of new manufacturers appeared. In Paterson, New Jersey, the Paterson Vehicle Company began making a line of diners under the "Silk City" marque (so named because of the town's bustling silk trade). Nearby in Newark, accountant Samuel Kullman quit P. J. Tierney and Sons and hung out his own shingle (he took Joseph Fodero, former metal-shop foreman for Tierney, with him). The trend continued, and by the end of the decade, the New England region—especially New York and New Jersey—was an unabashed hive of diner activity.

With all of the new eateries opening up, one of the age-old problems that confronted the diner man came into sharp focus: serving women! Since the dawn of the lunch wagon, diners faced a certain difficulty when it came to appealing to the ladies.

JULES DINER
In spite of the railroad car look of many diners, owners have added their own special touch to make a diner look more homey. Planter boxes, flowers, and handmade signs are all part of the effect. There's no place like home. *Jonathan Yonan ©1999*

TUMBLE INN INTERIOR
The city of Lynn, Massachusetts, is rich in diner history. During the 1940s, the Tumble Inn was a popular eatery where stools and counter seating ruled the day. Here, in the typical linear arrangement of the American diner, was the quintessential place where the weary traveler could, over time, pour down gallons of hot coffee and pounds of homemade pie. *Courtesy of the Lynn Historical Society*

"NEVER TOUCHED US"
The only building which was un-
damaged in the center of the fire zone.
Chelsea Mass.

Even during those uninhibited days of the flappers and speakeasies, women seldom patronized diners. They wanted no part of the unrefined atmosphere that they imagined occupied the inside of a typical eatery. They weren't that far off the mark: Diners often played host to foul language, cigar smoke, chewing tobacco, and the obligatory spittoon. Soiled clothing, ill manners, and bawdy talk were all too common in these beaneries where too many uncivilized men sat elbow-to-elbow to eat.

Nevertheless, diner operators craved the female business and tried everything they could to attract the fairer sex. In the big cities, some of

NEVER TOUCHED DINER

The Never Touched Diner (formerly the Vienna Cafe) is so named because of a particularly devastating event. Back in the early 1900s, a good portion of downtown Chelsea, Massachusetts, burned to the ground—save one very lucky diner. As the name paid homage to the catastrophe, it helped create a great reputation for the place. *Courtesy of Larry Cultrera*

them tried advertising flyers distributed to local businesses or used men they could hire as walking billboards. Some tried to spruce up the diner exterior with a half-hearted treatment of flower pots and other shrubbery.

More serious operators concentrated on keeping their places spic-and-span. Savvy diner guys figured out that the ladies liked nothing better than an immaculate kitchen (like their own at home), clean dishes, polished counters, sparkling tableware, and clean floors. They also liked it if their

TRANSPORTING THE DINERS

After diners lost their own wheels and grew in size and stature, the business of transporting them became integral to the industry. While railroad trains were sometimes used to move these dining structures over long distances, it was the many trucking operations of America that delivered them on short hops to their intended site of business. *Coolstock ©1999*

HI-WAY DINER

Located in Holyoke, Massachusetts, this Hi-Way diner was one in a proposed chain. In 1928, a group called the Hi-Way Diners Club of New England was formed in Springfield, Massachusetts, to create "a chain of better dining cars throughout the United States." The majority were to be located along national highways. The group chose Brill Steel Diners, a line of railroad-style food cars made by the Wason Manufacturing Company (a subsidiary of the J. G. Brill Company in Philadelphia) as its diner supplier. *From the Collection of Henry Ford Museum and Greenfield Village*

serving man looked good. A grubby apron, dirty fingernails, and a cigarette dangling from the mouth weren't images that won a gal's confidence.

Most problematic was the seating arrangement typical of the diner. While stools were adequate for truckers sporting blue jeans or businessmen wearing slacks, they were very uncomfortable for any woman wearing a dress. During the 1920s, a more formal standard of wardrobe prevailed and people seldom left the house donning the kind of casual clothes worn today (activewear fashions didn't exist). Most important, the etiquette of the day deemed it unladylike for a woman to straddle a diner stool.

For this reason, diner operators looked for ways to fit in a few tiny tables and, later, permanently installed booths. Because of space considerations, they installed these private areas in a single line down the length of the car, at one side,

near the windows (so passersby could see people eating). As a side effect, added booths demanded more than 4 extra feet from the width of a diner, causing them to grow in size.

Before too long, diner owners adorned their buildings with signs or painted on the slogan, "Booths For Ladies." Similarly, many adopted the practice of naming their diner with the feminine prefix, "Miss." Cold titles like the "City Lunch" or "Joe's Grill" didn't say much to the ladies. To exude more friendliness, names like the "Miss Worcester" or "Miss Bellows Falls" (painted in a fancy Old English-style of lettering) became the new fashion.

Although not a documented fact, some historians believe that diners acquired this female personae so that women would feel more welcome. It still remains a mystery, however, as to why the

RITE-BITE LUNCH ON WHEELS
The Rite-Bite Lunch was an elaborately decorated P. J. Tierney Sons creation, built in New Rochelle, New York. It made the trip to Philadelphia, Pennsylvania, on a small set of pneumatic tires, a grand feat, considering that the automobile was not yet perfected. As diners became larger and larger, this delivery process would become more difficult. *Courtesy of the Atwater Kent Museum*

AMERICAN EAGLE CAFE
Built in Worcester, Massachusetts, by the Worcester Lunch Car Company, the American Eagle Cafe (serial number 200) rolled out in the year 1907 and opened for business on Myrtle Street, behind the Worcester post office. Philip Duprey and Granville Stoddard were chief principles in the company with big business ideas. They bought out diner maker Wilfred Barriere in 1906 and took control of the local diner-making market. *Courtesy of the E. B. Luce Corporation*

diner operators used the unattached form of the title instead of the married form, "Mrs." Quite possibly, it was to keep the interest alive from the male segment of the market.

Eventually, all of this effort paid off. As the years went by, women slowly accepted the diner as a place where they could eat in relative comfort. Just like the men folk, they became regulars, brought their kids, and became equal partners in the diner enjoyment. In the years to come, women would jump to the other side of the counter and take regular jobs in many of these coffee shops, hash houses, and grills. During World War II, the diner icon known as the waitress would make her appearance.

Until that time, diners mobilized and took to the roadways, spreading the good news of fresh coffee and an affordable square meal far and wide. Out in the hinterlands, it was often the diner that fed travelers, offered a moment of respite, and slaked their thirst. Long before chain stores like Howard Johnson's colored the byways with their many flavors of ice cream, it was the generic diner that complemented roadside service businesses.

By the end of the 1920s, it wasn't uncommon to see wayside businesses such as gasoline stations

THE CHIEF DINER
"For Fine Foods"
DURANGO, COLORADO

THE CHIEF DINER INTERIOR

As diners became more popular, roadside entrepreneurs tried almost every angle they could think of to pack in the customers. Before it was considered politically incorrect to do so, some patterned their operations after Indian themes. The Chief Diner in Durango, Colorado, was a prime example. Outside, a large Indian Chief sign lit up the night, while inside, distinctive Indian decor stirred the imagination.
Courtesy of Roger Jackson

or tourist cabins augment their range of services by adding a diner. Since diners already came assembled and ready to go, it was easy for any operator with the cash to add on food service, fast. It was quite a lucrative proposition, as the automobile was now king. Scores of Americans were hitting the roads in quest of tourism, escape, and adventure. Like the city workers of Providence so long ago, they all required sustenance. They found it roadside—in the diner.

One of the most-documented examples of this move toward highway dining appeared in 1928. That year, a group called the Hi-Way Diners Club of New England Inc. was formed in Springfield,

Massachusetts. The goal of the organization was to create "a chain of better dining cars throughout the United States," with the intent that the majority take up residence along the national highways. Club members believed that while the state of America's roads and the amenities offered there were getting better all the time, there was room for improvement in the area of dining.

For the anticipated chain, Hi-Way Diners chose Brill Steel Diners, a line of railroad-style food cars made by the Wason Manufacturing Company, a subsidiary of the J. G. Brill Company of Philadelphia, Pennsylvania. The company was a streetcar and rail car maker and had experience when it

PERFECT DINER

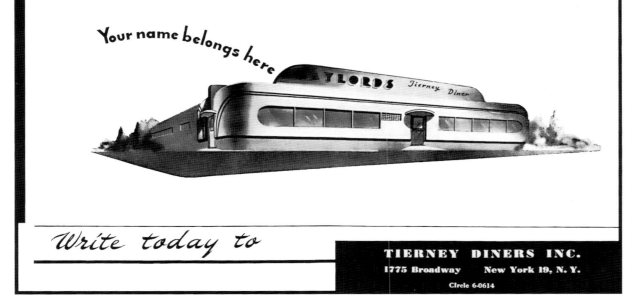

KNOW WHY IT'S *EASY* TO OWN
YOUR OWN TIERNEY DINER

Your name belongs here

Write today to

TIERNEY DINERS INC.
1775 Broadway   New York 19, N. Y.
Circle 6-0614

THE PERFECT DINER

The Perfect Diner (most likely a Wilfred Barriere model) is a good example of how the early lunch wagon evolved to become a full-scale restaurant. After the early 1900s, diners began to grow in length; however, they still clung to their fancy window glass, barrel roof, and wagon-like profile. Still, using two doors for ingress and egress was unusual. Most diners of the Golden Age would rely on a single center- or end-mounted portal. *From the Collections of the Worcester Historical Museum, Worcester, Massachusetts*

TIERNEY STREAMLINED ADVERTISEMENT

Tierney ventured into the realm of streamlining during the 1930s and placed color advertisements in industry magazines. Back in those days, restaurant proprietors wanted roadside buildings that looked fast. Not only did the look conjure up distinct feelings of modernism, it evoked a sense of speedy service and efficiency, two important diner attributes. *Preziosi Postcards*

COTTAGE AND DINER

Located on U.S. Highway 15A near Fayetteville, North Carolina, Thompson's Cottage Court and Diner was a typical example of the roadside lodging operation that paired up with the business of serving food. This tiny diner appears to be a former trolley car (notice the front-mounted headlamp) that was built directly into one of the sleeping cabins. *Courtesy Brian Butko*

came to space-efficient structures. The company catalog said it all: "Brill Steel Diners are going on locations everywhere in rapidly increasing numbers. A profitable asset to any gas filling station."

Adding fuel to the train-cum-diner controversy, Brill's catalog went on about how they "introduced some of the features characteristic of the palatial railroad diner which is so popular." It was a fact: Brill diners had monitor roofs (with a small side deck sash and tiny vent windows), just like those found on the early trolleys. Like the railroad box car, they used a metal framework and skins,

finished with a coat of lacquer. Eight "full-vision" windows (that patrons could raise and lower) came with screens. At each end, a door faced front. The only thing lacking was a conductor who stood outside and yelled "All Aboard!"

And that's exactly what most of America did. In great numbers, they jumped aboard the diners and made them part of their lives. At breakfast, truck drivers and longshoremen wolfed down plates of bacon and eggs between gulps of coffee and the chatter of road stories. At lunch, professional workers met associates for a quick bite to eat

THOMPSON'S COTTAGE COURT AND DINER
On U. S. 15A, Two Miles South of Fayetteville, North Carolina

DINER SKELETON CONSTRUCTION
Diner maker Wilfred Barriere constructed diners right alongside his Cleveland Avenue house in Worcester, Massachusetts. During the 1920s, the interior framework of diners was still made of wood, a material that was readily available and easy to fashion into a number of different configurations. *From the Collections of the Worcester Historical Museum, Worcester, Massachusetts*

BARRIERE'S PURPLE DINER
Constructed by Wilfred H. Barriere of Worcester, Massachusetts, the Purple Diner is an early example (probably the 1920s) of the typical diner arrangement that would soon dominate the industry. In most cases, manufacturers would mount the door at the center of the box and flank it with multiple windows. *From the Collections of the Worcester Historical Museum, Worcester, Massachusetts*

and lingered over the daily newspaper. In the afternoon, housewives met members of the coffee klatch for a piece of pie and gossip. Ever so slowly, the diner seduced the populace and worked itself into the popular culture of America.

At the center of this increased social interaction were affordability and convenience. For the most part, diners were a good value and served a grade of food that made it quite natural for customers to open their wallets and dig into their purses. It was considerably easy to "hang out" and relax when you never had to worry about high prices or appearances. Besides, people in the cities recognized the diner as the late-night place to be, aided by those that kept the coffee on 24 hours a day.

With the public hooked, the diner chugged onward through the years of the Great Depression and entered the 1930s virtually unscathed. Sure, a few outfits went bankrupt here and there or saw a dramatic drop in business; but overall, the majority survived much of the economic tumult. The faithful never wavered in their belief that the diner was a recession-proof business.

They had good reason for their optimism. The general public just couldn't get enough of these novel eateries where they could scarf down cheap, good-tasting food and quaff their favorite beverages. A quick look-see around the inside of any neighborhood diner proved it. Everyone took part in the informal diner's club, including milkmen, chauffeurs, debutantes, teamsters, young men-about-town, students, streetcar motormen, messenger boys, policemen, businessmen, truck drivers, salesmen, and other food operators. Regardless of place, membership was open to all.

Devoid of a social caste system, diners became commercial neutral zones where both the down-and-out, the middle class, and even the well-off broke bread under the very same roof. All the layers of society rubbed elbows at the counter and dropped coins in the jukebox. Backstage, a diverse range of nationalities were able to own a diner and make their mark in the industry.

When one considers that the diners of the early teens and 1920s were the hub of social activity, the core of culinary convenience, and a visible example of capitalism at its best, it's easy to believe that the diner was the American dream. In less than 40 years, the low-cost, come-as-you-are diner rose up from its humble lunch wagon beginnings to become a representation of freedom itself. In America, the diner was democracy.

THE DINER STORE

As part of Jerry Berta's ever-growing Dinerland in Rockford, Michigan, the Diner Store (a 1947 O'Mahony) features "No food, Just Art." It started out life as Uncle Bob's Diner in Flint, Michigan, until it fell into disrepair. Berta found the beauty in 1987 and set about to restore it. He accomplished that task, and today Uncle Bob's has a new lease on life. *Jerry Berta ©1999*

CHAPTER THREE

STAINLESS STEEL VISIONS AND NEON DREAMS

The Golden Age of American Diners

"Want to be your own boss? You'd surely like a business which has been thoroughly tested by many reputable people all over the country ever since the turn of the century. You'd prefer a small, individual business. A closely knit organization which is as simple to run and control as A B C. Then you owe it to yourself, in all fairness, to fully investigate all the possibilities in owning and operating a Silk City Diner. Want security for yourself and family? Surely you do. And you can have it now and for years to come. A very reasonable investment can supply you with one of the highest regular net profits available in any business—bar none. It provides an opportunity to start earning an attractive income in your own town, or, if you prefer, in some other locality. You will be a respected member of the community. And your family will be assured of ample security in the future."

The Silk City Diner brochure
Paterson Vehicle Company, circa 1950s

By 1932, figures showed that there were an estimated 4,000 portable lunchrooms operating in the United States. These eateries weren't your father's lunch wagon by any stretch. That year, the *Literary Digest* reported that the lunch wagon was no longer a wagon at all, "but a pretentious, semi-permanent, bijou restaurant, designed by engineers familiar with Pullman-car and ship architecture." It was an apt description, as the diner companies began to implement features that made the diner more efficient inside and more beautiful outside.

Starting with the early days of the Depression and lasting until the onset of World War II (and continuing thereafter), this nation's diner builders developed improved, innovative designs. During this revolutionary era, the ultimate discipline known as "industrial design" became the preference when making manufactured goods. Suddenly, industry deemed consumer products more marketable if they took on a sophisticated look. Whether it was a toaster, an automobile, or a commercial roadside structure—its outward appearance was held as more important than its function.

Ideally suited to this new philosophy, automobiles grew gracefully rounded fenders, sprouted teardrop taillamps, and gained curved-window profiles. In 1934, Chrysler debuted a motor carriage called the "Airflow," a vehicle with rounded corners and streamlined features that evoked an image of gliding through the wind. Alexander Klemin, the director of New York's Guggenheim School of Aeronautics, referred to it as "perhaps the most beautiful product of the machine age." In America, this was the unofficial beginning of the streamlined era.

As the nation rushed to redesign products in tune with the hum of this new machine age, automotive-related enterprises also adopted

SOUTHPORT DINER
Kullman took the art of diner design to new heights when it began building stainless steel-and-porcelain panel-striped diners like the Southport Diner (which operated in Connecticut). Here's a masterpiece of diner construction with eye-catching looks, a jaunty stance, and so much style you can taste it. *Pedar Ness ©1999*

LAWRENCE DINER
Streamlined Moderne. Suddenly, once-static buildings looked like they were ready to lift off, hit the road, and join the other traffic.

Fortunately, designers included the diner in this roadside retooling. The architects of the age smoothed the characteristic angled corners and hard edges, and within a few short years, roadside restaurants that once looked like beached railroad box cars slipped on more svelte, tailored shells. Aerodynamic streamlined styling defined the exterior shroud.

As businesses scrambled to conform to this new mobile look, American industry made some tremendous manufacturing strides. Suddenly, materials that were at one time difficult (and costly) to make became much easier to manufacture. The industrial advancements created a life-sized Erector Set filled with exciting new construction options. To the delight of the food industry, many of these materials were applied to building restaurants—and most specifically, the diner.

Armed with new techniques and materials, diner designers went to work on the quadrangular diner building of the teens and 1920s and began to work their art. In this quest to create the

LAWRENCE DINER

The time: the 1970s. The place: Queens, New York. This was the Lawrence Diner, a neighborhood hot spot dripping in stainless steel and sweating of atmosphere. Is there any doubt that this joint played host to a rogue's gallery of customers, characters, and other late-night players? Turn up the soundtrack—the theme music from *Saturday Night Fever*. *Pedar Ness ©1999*

the appearance of speed. Along the roadways, service stations and gasoline pumps were transformed from hard-edged boxes into blunt, tidy monoliths. Bus stations, airline terminals, suburban theaters, car dealerships, and motor hotels took on the accelerated characteristics of

SILVER DINER

Years before the new Silver Diner chain of modern retro diners existed, the real thing was reaping the bounty of the roadways. Hooking in the drive-by customers on Connecticut's Berlin Turnpike near Hartford, some thought that this stainless steel-and-neon-banded monolith would last forever. *Pedar Ness ©1999*

ultimate streamlined dream, their goal was single-minded: give the diner a make over into the speeding image of the modern passenger train, plane, or automobile.

In 1932, Paramount Diners hung out its shingle in New Jersey and became the first East Coast diner manufacturer to blaze the trail with new materials. Paramount raised a few eyebrows among the diner men when it found new uses for an industrial material called Formica, a hard, laminated sheeting invented in 1913 by Herbert Faber and Daniel O'Conner. (This thin composite board was originally intended as a substitute "for mica," a naturally occurring insulating mineral used by industry and electronics.)

As a material to finish interiors, Formica was perfect: It afforded easy installation and tremendous durability. It was rigid, but flexible, and installers affixed it with glue or fasteners. Unlike the yearly varnishing or paintings demanded by wood, it held a smooth, colorful, water-resistant finish for years. Best of all, cleaning a year's accumulation of grease and nicotine was a snap. To make it look brand new, all it took was a quick wipe-down.

Before long, most of the other diner makers saw the future and joined the visionaries at Paramount, using Formica wherever they could. At first, it found widespread use as a ceiling material and replaced wood, porcelain enamel, and metal. When the company produced a new version that resisted cigarette burns, Formica quickly became the industry's countertop and tabletop material. By that time, Formica boasted a rainbow of colors and an assortment of attractive silk-screened and inlaid patterns.

JOE'S DINER

Joe's Diner is one of those diminutive Kullman Juniors, complete with a corner entrance and acres of bright stainless steel on the exterior. Flaunting its gleaming armor in the shadow of the freeway, this Seymour, Connecticut, eatery knew a good slogan when it heard one. During the late 1970s, "Time to Eat" was the call to motorists speeding by on the superslab above.
Pedar Ness ©1999

EAT AT ZIP'S

Day or night, you can see Zip's "Eat" sign from miles away. It's a great message—because after all, isn't that what you do inside a diner? Billed as "New England's Finest Dining Car," this 1954 Jerry O'Mahony still charms the dreamers and fills their bellies with good grub in Dayville, Connecticut.
Pedar Ness ©1999

One particular Formica pattern, characterized by a graphic repetition of a boomerang-shaped chevron, became the most widely recognized (and most loved) by present-day diner aficionados. This was the successful pattern they called "Skylark," a diner counter standard that Brooks Stevens designed during the 1950s (reproduction diners of today routinely use this style to achieve what they believe is the right nostalgic effect).

Inspired by the many changes and the wealth of new materials, other diner builders came out of the mahogany to add their own entry into the roadside beauty contest. It was 1933 when Joseph Fodero left his post at the Kullman Dining Car Company with an itch to start his own. As a metal shop foreman, he knew what it took to build an attractive diner and had the skills to see it through. So, with more ideas than manufacturing facilities, Fodero began to build his own exciting line of dining cars right alongside his home in Bloomfield, New Jersey.

As detailed by industry magazines like the *Diner*, Fodero produced a trio of magnificent styles that redefined the industry. With its rounded corners,

monitor roof, and duo-color finish, his most memorable design gained the description "terra cotta." Taking its name from the profusion of steel-and-porcelain–enameled panels on the exterior, this variation featured a row of windows, rounded at each end, much like busses of the day. Stainless steel became the material of choice for window and roof trim, to cover seams, and for the center door, which had a porthole. Each diner's name was baked into the porcelain panels right at the factory, using the bold art deco lettering style known as "Broadway."

Fodero crafted another captivating style that relied on a linear arrangement of "fluted porcelain." Using the same footprint as the latter, this model turned heads with dozens of shaped, semicircular strips of colored porcelain panels interlaced with stainless. These alternating bands ran a vertical

course around the structure's perimeter. The visual effect gained by the combination of polished and glazed metal was mesmerizing. Prospective buyers took one look at the ads and had to have it.

A third "streamlined" design relied on the same materials. This diner was similar in shape to both the terra-cotta and the fluted porcelain styles, the main difference being that the strips of porcelain and stainless steel ran horizontally across the diner body. When Fodero used two colors of porcelain in this configuration, he called it the "modernistic" version.

Not surprisingly, the restaurateurs and customers of the 1930s responded well to the bright, optimistic designs. Through no small coincidence, most of America's diners fell into the four classifications typified by the Fodero line, both before and after World War II. Not averse to following the diner crowd, competing companies such as DeRaffele (which also opened in 1933), O'Mahony, Kullman, Mountain View, and Silk City built diners in one or more of the aforementioned styles.

At last, the diner was a roadside structure that projected a personality all its own. It wasn't really a railroad car anymore, and it wasn't really an ordinary building. One thing was certain, however; the diner was a unique edifice that defied the usual attempts at classification. With well-balanced proportions, and ample room inside, it was sleek, colorful, attractive, and spoke the streetside dialect of an energetic new era.

In 1936 the J. B. Judkins Company of Merrimac, Massachusetts, presented the industry with one of the most original diner designs ever. Before the Depression years began, Judkins specialized in the construction of custom automobile bodies for affluent customers. When hard times slowed down the flow of orders, the company looked to related markets. Coincidentally, building diners meshed well with its stock of tools and facilities, so J. B. Judkins decided to build portable eateries.

As indicated by historical documents and patent records, the first model produced used the plans of Bertron G. Harley, a well-respected boat

GOOD FOOD COLD BEER
A rooftop sign reading "Good Food Cold Beer" was the only identification and advertising seen on this unusual Perris, California, diner in the early days of the 1980s. The diner denizens who built this stretched train car weren't fooling around. It features a monitor-style roof with ample vent windows, curved ends with observation windows, and large, canopied picture windows at the front. All in all, a turquoise mirage for the traveler. *Pedar Ness ©1999*

OLE GEHMAN'S SIGN

Gehman's is a surviving example of a Silk City diner, a line of prefabricated eateries manufactured in Paterson, New Jersey. It's located on U.S Route 30, a half mile east of Route 896 in Ronk's, Pennsylvania. Look for the striking, vertical "Diner" sign. A true time warp awaits you. *Keith Baum ©1999*

builder and inventor from Maine who devised an unusual method to snap together diners from sectionalized blocks. Workmen constructed the 4-foot-wide diner segments ahead of time in the factory, allowing them to be trucked to building sites with unheard-of ease. Once delivered, the site installers joined together these modular segments (some had seats, counters, and other kitchen equipment) until they formed the proper length and diner arrangement specified by the customer.

In spite of the obvious delivery advantages and the novelty of construction, the modular diner method never displaced standard building methods. Perhaps it was the dowdy styling that limited the Sterling's popularity: Here was the same old monitor-style roof treatment and four-corner boxiness of the railroad car. Sure some windows were decked out with orange leaded-glass at the transom, but the barrel-vaulted ceiling was hardly an innovation.

For these reasons and more, demand was never that great and a general lack of enthusiasm convinced the company to take another direction. In 1939, Judkins surprised everyone when they jumped into the diner fast lane and patented a brand new unit called the Sterling Streamliner. This attention-getting structure was the brain-child of New York City inventor Roland Stickney.

STOP HERE FOR GOOD EATIN'

This Salem, Illinois, diner appears to be of the homemade variety. During the prewar years, many operators who couldn't afford to buy a premanufactured unit ventured out on their own and built their own idea of what a diner should be. Photographer Arthur Rothstein captured this timeless image for the Farm Security Administration in 1940. *Library of Congress*

Stickney's diner dream was a major departure from the norm. It looked like it was going somewhere even when it was standing still. Even so, the design was slightly derivative of railroad styling of that era. The well-traveled commuter and train passenger immediately recognized the Streamliner as a faithful copy of the legendary Burlington Zephyr, the 1934 streamlined locomotive built by the Edward G. Budd Company for the Chicago, Burlington, and Quincy Railroad. Only the tracks and passenger cars were missing.

As far as looks, the Sterling Streamliner had all of the attractive attributes of its track-bound cousin, minus the massive diesel engine. At the ends, the Streamliner copied the locomotive nose section, right down to the slant of the curved nose (the only item left out was the center-mounted train headlamp). Originally, Stickney planned for both ends to feature circular portholes, but the company saw fit to install thin, rectangular windows. On top of the round roof, a long, fin-like projection caught the gaze of traffic and provided space for neon lettering and other signage.

The Sterling Streamliners raced across America and became a modern representative for the dining car field. One of the most memorable streamlined installations was a single-ended unit that emerged from a fake railroad tunnel. (Its builders installed the kitchen inside.) In Houston, Texas, Emmett Simpson, a former steward on the Missouri & Pacific train line, opened one of these diners in 1940 (called Simpson's Diner), as did forward-thinking operators in New York state, Massachusetts, Rhode Island, and other New England regions. (Both the "Modern Diner" and the "My Tin Man Diner" are extant examples of the Sterling locomotive genre.)

Taking its cues from machine-age designers the likes of Raymond Loewy and Norman Bel Geddes, the diner emerged as a reincarnated version of the streamlined train car. As much as the American diner industry desperately tried to shake off the railroad

SALEM DINER INTERIOR

The city of Salem, Massachusetts, is where the motoring diner buff needs to travel to take supper inside a beautiful, original Sterling Streamliner. In terms of visual presence and interior design beauty, there's nothing like it. Could this be what the diners in heaven are like? *Ronald Saari ©1999*

AIRLINE DINER

Georges Claude discovered that when neon gas was electrically excited with high voltage, it glowed fiery red. He invented the corrosion-resistant electrode and patented the design in 1915. By the end of the 1930s, most gas stations, drugstores, drive-ins, and diners were bedecked in a kaleidoscope of electric color. A local landmark for all those arriving and departing by plane, the Airline Diner electrifies the darkness in Astoria, Queens, New York, near the LaGuardia Airport. *Pedar Ness ©1999*

RIVERSIDE DINER

Back in 1948, the local diner scene in Medford, Massachusetts, was characterized by Jerry O'Mahony diners like the Riverside. Within a few short years, all that changed. Diners were destined to look more and more like the bus parked out in front. Wood was on its way out and metals were to dominate. *Courtesy of Larry Cultrera*

connection, designers continued incorporating train-like features into their restaurant cars. Streamlining became the metaphor for adventure in traveling. What other form could better reflect the mercurial qualities of speed and modernity?

Apparently, there wasn't another style that did, as it didn't take long for other diner manufacturers to roll out their own version. Around the same time that Sterling turned heads with its speedy new look, the Worcester Lunch Car Company came out with a train-styled streamliner of its own. It was a headache for the company to build, considering all of the compound curves and specialized techniques required (making cabinets and fitting woodwork to the multitude of curves was maddening work). Although the company hawked the prototype model in issues of *The Diner*, actual construction was limited to only two diners.

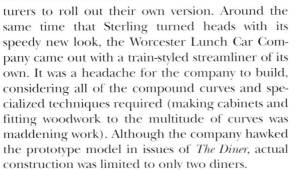

But that wasn't the end of Worcester's entry into the world of streamlining. The company decided to concentrate on a simpler version that provided the same look, yet required less effort to build. This particular model dropped the round, complex ends in favor of slanted bulkheads that provided the illusion of speed without all the cost. Later, Worcester used an angled style of italic lettering for the exterior name, further enhancing the illusion of forward momentum. Strange as it was, the railroad mind-set prevailed. Some of the diner models built in this configuration went by names like "Pullman" and "Streamliner."

Like it or not, the strange alliance with trains continued and reached its zenith when stainless steel took over the diner exterior. By the end of the 1930s, the clean, scrubbed look of stainless steel emerged as the mainstay of American diner

SUNNYSIDE UP III

In Lowell, Massachusetts, this modified diner (possibly an original Worcester) went by the name of the Chateau Diner during its "blue" period. When it slipped into its "red" period, it tickled the eyeballs as the Sunnyside Up III. With all of that out of its system, it became the Trolley Stop, a pizza joint. The streamlined panels are gone and the ends have been rounded to make it look more like a trolley car. Clerestory windows that light up from the inside finish the makeover. *Pedar Ness ©1999*

industry architecture and evolved to define the standard diner "look." In his publication, *The American Diner: Then and Now*, Richard Gutman presents a believable case (synopsized here) for the adoption of this material.

The story begins with Erwin Fedkenheuer, a German immigrant sheet-metal worker who had a particularly skillful knack for bending steel. Fedkenheuer apparently got his big break during the early 1930s. At the time, he was working for S. Blickman Inc., a New Jersey manufacturer of food service equipment. Art Sieber, then the president of Paramount Diners, asked him to fabricate a few stainless steel coffee urns for his company. Erwin then performed all of the work with Paramount's tools and facilities.

While at the diner factory, Fedkenheuer spied a diner that was in the process of being built and admired its construction. After looking it over more closely, he commented that "using a little bit of stainless steel would look nice." Sieber concurred with the off-hand remark and entreated Fedkenheuer to fashion some window trim pieces on the spot. He did, and the rest is history.

After Paramount installed the completed diner, some competing diner makers dropped by for coffee—and to take a closer look at the new model. As the tale goes, they were all quite interested in the

KIRK'S DINER

"Wait a minute Scotty, don't beam me up; we just passed a place called Kirk's Diner! Beam down a reconnaissance crew and meet me at the front vestibule; we're going in for some hot coffee and apple pie!" This isn't a scene from another world, but a glimpse of stainless steel roadside New Jersey at its finest, a blast from the past (circa 1976) along Route 22. *Pedar Ness ©1999*

WORKING KINGS-X COUNTERMEN

Kings-X was a Wichita, Kansas–based diner operation that was spun off from the White Castle chain by a former employee, Frank King. Inside these gleaming white, porcelain-enameled buildings, dapper young countermen in white shirts and black bow ties served some of the best American burgers (small, steamed sandwiches topped off with grilled onions) to eager car customers of the 1940s and 1950s. *Local History Section, Wichita Public Library*

THE OLYMPIA DINER

The old highway leaving Hartford, Connecticut, was also known as the Berlin Turnpike. Before the big freeways, it was a melting pot of diners. Up and down the strip, dining cars of every make and model called to the motorist from the blacktop. It was a language of neon, stainless steel, and aromatic vapors. Today, most of the words have been lost. To light the way at dusk, only a few diners like the Olympia power up the neon. *Pedar Ness ©1999*

application of stainless steel. All of the diner men returned to their respective factories clutching detailed sketches of Fedkenheuer's work drawn on their napkins. Designers soon planted the seed, and it wouldn't take long before stainless steel was being used both inside and outside.

Capitalizing on the growing excitement for the new steel designs, Fedkenheuer left the S. Blickman company and joined Paramount (thus began a career that culminated in the most spectacular diner designs of all time). With Fedkenheuer working as the lead sheet metal man, Paramount pioneered new uses for the material, replacing the back bar tiles with gleaming panels of steel. Kitchen counters were changed from wood into stainless, as were storage cabinets and exposed trim. With polished metal comprising almost every surface, the diner became an oversized appliance.

While some were content to build diners with an exterior made of alternating bands of porcelain-clad steel and stainless, the gleam of polished metal was irresistible to Paramount. Before the United

States entered World War II, stainless steel crept from the inside of the diner to completely cover the outside of the diner. Paramount led the diner field, taking the techniques of stainless steel construction and turning them into a much-envied art form.

It was more than just a cold application of bent sheet metal: Company artisans forced the inner beauty hidden within the steel up to the surface. It was painstaking work, as one mistake resulted in a ruined piece and the need to start over.

Craftsmen literally worked magic with their tools, bending and shaping the metal to yield patterns that were pleasing to the eye. This visual repertoire included vertical creases, quilted fields, and dramatic sunbursts. At the most extreme, craftsmen burnished a double row of circles into panels and then installed them on the exterior. Now, the diner was beautiful, striking, and durable, protected by a rustproof armor that had the moxie to resist the harsh punishment of moisture and everyday use. With undeniable eye-appeal and pizzazz, stainless steel *was* the diner.

Ironically, the very same material that made the diner such a roadside beauty was causing a few problems in transport. With all of the stainless steel panels and other miscellaneous metal pieces, new diners were tipping the scales like none before them. Transporting these overweight assemblies became a major part of buying a diner, considering the high costs of truck and rail freight. It was tricky work, spawning an entire industry of movers that made the delivery of diners a specialized business.

But whether a diner came in the stainless steel, terra-cotta, or just plain wood configuration, many factors contributed to the final costs of the delivery. Some of the more important points included the condition of the undercarriage, shipping distance, obstructions from utility wires, weight over bridges, and the various permits required by the many cities and states along the delivery route (what was basically a tax levied to access the roads).

On the long-distance end, matters were just as serious: In order to negotiate the tunnels and curves, and to satisfy all of the numerous constraints associated with the rail lines, pre-assembled eateries were feasible only if they adhered to specific widths and lengths. This was a problem for the nation's diner builders, as the demand for bigger and bigger eateries was growing. Every time a new model came out, diner customers cried out for even more room and more features.

To address this three-tiered dilemma of weight, size, and delivery, Paramount led the way when it won a patent for a "split diner" in 1941. As evidenced by company sales literature, this clever variation on normal construction methods called for the manufacturer to build a diner in two (and sometimes more) sections. Movers could transport

THE 11TH STREET DINER

Miami, Florida's 11th Street Diner (which used to be the Olympic in Wilkes-Barre, Pennsylvania) exemplifies the work of the master sheet metal artisan, a la the Paramount brand. Decades before it was fashionable to encase commercial buildings in sand-colored brick (in order to make them blend into the roadside), American diner manufacturers did all they could to make a diner structure stand out from the roadside. *Marty Lineen Jr. ©1999*

each of these slices with more facility than one larger piece. It worked. With split diner construction, it was possible to circumvent the transit restrictions. With this unique innovation in place, the delivery of oversized diners wasn't a problem anymore and giant eateries were on the way to towns across the United States.

Company sales diagrams showed that the separating split ran lengthwise, right down the center of the diner. The problem of rigidity was solved by using a unique design where the two halves were joined together. This formed a single, continuous structure without vertical supports. Under the floor and along the split, a rigid channel and truss arrangement supported the joined edges. One half of the prebuilt hunk held booths, stools, and counter, while the other half contained the kitchen, cabinets, and back bar.

With delivery concerns addressed and the diner exterior revamped, the restaurant industry looked like it was in for some heady times. Unfortunately, all of the innovation wasn't enough to sustain the industry during the meager war years. Major car manufacturers cut back on the production of vehicles, as did industries that relied on the raw materials necessary for the war effort. Steel was in high demand to make tanks, guns, bombs, and warplanes. Building more dining cars wasn't vital to defense.

For this reason, the diner business experienced some lean times from 1942 on, as did many
continued on page 86

SALEM DINER EXTERIOR
The Salem Diner is a combination of art deco elegance and the raw power exhibited by the planes, trains, and automobiles of the 1930s. This Massachusetts landmark opened its portals on July 3, 1941, and attracted more crowds than the famous witch burnings did. Workers toiled for three days and nights until the crowds thinned out and the door was locked to keep them out. Today, it's still popular—a bona fide roadside novelty. *Ronald Saari ©1999*

NEW IDEAL DINER
The New Ideal Diner is just the kind of picture that one would find if they looked up the word diner in the dictionary. With searing letters of orange-red neon and bands of dazzling stainless to reflect the wondrous light, this diner has what it takes to make passing drivers stomp on the brakes and park it. It is located in Aberdeen, Maryland. *Ronald Saari ©1999*

DESTINY WITH ROSIE'S

ROSIE'S DINER/DINERLAND USA

4500 14 Mile Road ★ Rockford, Michigan

If you doubt the power of fate, don't talk to Jerry Berta. Jerry, known for his ceramic-and-neon diner replicas, cites evidence of fate's intervention in his own life with great enthusiasm. As a young artist attending Wayne State University in Detroit, Michigan, he had no idea that his future would be in diner art. As a matter of fact, his teachers went out of their way to warn him that "you can't make a living as an artist!" Fortunately, he didn't listen.

After receiving his bachelor of fine arts degree from Wayne State, he met and married Madeline Kaczmarczyk. Together, they established the Funky and Functional Pottery. Jerry created works for the "funky" portion of the business, while Madeline created the "functional" items. They proceeded to sell their unique line of pottery at arts and crafts fairs across the country. As fate would have it, Berta made a pivotal detour on one such trip to New Jersey.

On their way to an exhibit, Jerry and his wife decided to conduct a quick photo expedition of the Jersey roadside. By pure chance, they wound up in Little Ferry, right in front of Rosie's diner. Smitten with the sight, Jerry began taking photos, only to be shooed away by an irate cook. Although he didn't know it at the time,

ROSIE'S DINER PREP
The New Jersey location of Rosie's Farmland Diner was well known among all those who traversed a path through the Garden State. While she was made nationally famous by memorable paper towel commercials, Rosie's held a certain measure of fame with her loyal and devoted customers. For an American diner, that's what true, lasting notoriety is all about. *Jerry Berta ©1999*

Jerry was standing in front of a famous diner, a restaurant icon catapulted to stardom by the Bounty paper towel commercials of the late 1970s.

It "looked like an appliance, a toaster, all round and curvy . . . it was love at first sight," remembers Jerry. The rounded lines, stainless steel, and glass bricks knocked him out. He returned to Michigan, photos in hand and an idea in mind. Back in his studio, he set to work creating his first ceramic diner piece. Like the real thing, it had all the cool stuff, including oval doors, curvy glass bricks, and rounded roof. As a finishing touch, he crowned his diner with a neon halo and rooftop sign.

Jerry's new obsession with the diner form didn't end there. In 1986, he purchased a vacant lot off Highway 14 with plans to build a bigger studio. One year later, the pieces of his life fell into place when he bought and moved Uncle Bob's Diner of Flint, Michigan (a 1947 Jerry O'Mahony) to his tract of land in Rockford. With care, the vintage eatery was restored and promptly put to use as a combination gallery and studio. Dubbed the Diner Store by Jerry, it became a visible symbol of his art.

Curiously enough, the Diner Store sparked an interest in motorists who thought they had found the perfect place

Rising above all the mishaps, the diner arrived late in January and landed in front of Berta's Diner Store. It was in good shape but needed work. The first order of business was the removal of the harvest-gold counter installed by Proctor and Gamble for the Bounty commercials. Jerry replaced the garish surface with a metal-edged, textured, pink Formica counter. He also trashed the exterior doors and replaced them with oval, art deco beauties.

One year later, these classic doors were swung open for the official grand-opening. Hoping for 50 customers that first day, Jerry was amazed to find a line outside. By 10 o'clock in the morning, there were 50 curious and hungry people waiting to be fed. That day, more than 300 pair of feet crossed Rosie's threshold. Jerry's publicity secret? Just a simple banner strung up in front of the doors.

to eat. This steady stream of travelers who dropped by for a bite to eat prompted Jerry to place a sign in the window that read, "No Food, Just Art, Truckers Welcome." For many of the visitors, the lack of food was disappointing, but a few browsed through the gallery. As Jerry reminisces, "these truckers would otherwise never have stopped at a gallery, but they loved this one."

In 1989, fate once again dealt Jerry a new hand. This time, it brought him full circle. While traveling to New York City for a crafts show, he recalled the paradigm shift that resulted from his visit to Rosie's 10 years earlier, and he decided to look up his muse. To his dismay, the diner was closed for the day. Following the script of his past visit, he began taking photographs.

Just then, Ralph Carrado (owner of Rosie's) opened the back door and invited Jerry in for a cup of coffee. The two chatted for a while and Jerry related his love for diners, his diner art, and his own vintage diner. When Ralph quipped, "you want to buy another one?" Jerry didn't hesitate. The 1946 Paramount was slated for demolition. Rosie's, the inspiration that spurred Jerry into diner art would be his. Destiny? Ask Jerry and he'll shoot you a resounding, "Yes!"

Rosie's move from Little Ferry to Rockford, Michigan, prompted intense media coverage. CNN was on hand to cover the event, which began January 13, 1990. The Associated Press ran stories about Rosie's final days, while local radio and television reporters followed the diner's progress as it trundled toward its new destination. The move wasn't without incident: An engine fire delayed the entourage in Ohio and 10 flat tires along the way wreaked havoc. Through it all, Jerry kept his unflappable humor.

Not one to rest on his laurels, Jerry set out to construct more attractions for his ad hoc amusement park, including an 18-hole miniature golf course. Naturally, it took on the theme of "food and art." First, you play through breakfast—bacon and eggs and a spilled cup of coffee, the thing that made Rosie's famous. Then it's on to lunch and dinner. The hardest hole of all is the one called "Art," a colorful artist's palette. After playing a round, customers often remark that "the food is easy but the art is hard!"

A couple other diners took up residence on Jerry's four acres, including an eye-popping Silk City (named the Deluxe Diner) and a nice homemade model. What was once just an empty field is now known as Dinerland, a fun, family-style recreation complex. Jerry, the self-described "big ol' goofy guy in a big ol' goofy world" holds court as the benevolent king of a real-life diner world. How does he describe the essence of his realm? Simple: "Eat and buy art! Rosie's is art, the whole building is art, the whole complex is art! The food had to be good to pay for it!"

Most Beautiful
D I N E R
in Chicago

EAT

BURLINGTON DINER. 4183 the Burlington

RESTAURANT CIGARETTES

GOOD FOOD

QUICK SERVICE

THE BURLINGTON DINER

The Burlington Diner was touted by its owners as "The Most Beautiful Diner in Chicago." This model looks so much like a railroad car, it's quite possible that an actual rail dining car was retrofitted for the purpose. *Courtesy of Roger Jackson*

continued from page 83

other related businesses. With few orders for new diners coming in and scant material with which to construct them, a few diner makers went out of business. Those who prepared for the austerity measures of the times sustained themselves with work in the military end of the manufacturing business. Others managed to squeeze through with the diner orders already in hand.

The hard times didn't last forever. When the war finally ended in 1948, American diner construction gradually picked up where it left off and slowly resumed to normal. With gasoline rationing fading into memory, the fuel pumps once again flowed freely. Long-distance and recreational automobile travel—and the endless sessions of eating out that accompanied it—were back. The diner business rose to the occasion and rebounded with a vengeance.

By this time, many returning servicemen had formulated their own plans and were eager to get into the auspicious business of roadside eats. Next to a red Thunderbird, a new wife, and your own tract house, there was a special aura connected with owning your "own joint." And—after enduring the many hardships of war—America's ex-military men didn't view the idea of making it on your own with a restaurant, a diner, as such a big deal.

Concurrently, the sons of the prominent diner makers returned home to continue their fathers' fight for market share. With the diner industry renewed, a host of companies received an infusion of new blood. This was great for the advancement of the industry, as new companies were spun off from some of the existing diner names. With the economy picking up, the American diner industry was back on track and poised to experience another renaissance.

By that time, aesthetic tastes and the rate of commuter travel had changed faster than roadside architecture could keep up with it. Streamlining was still in general use, but no longer held red-hot appeal. Jaded by the new, emerging technology of warfare, the public no longer regarded rounded corners, angled ends, and slanted lettering as looking all that fast. Ready for a new direction, diner designers promptly moved on to styling more indicative of postwar prosperity.

As shown by many examples of the era, diner builders backed away from the programmatic design concepts and concentrated on the more practical points of architecture: durability and lasting beauty. Designers took a lot of their inspiration from the automotive industry, copying the look of

decorative elements like heavy bumper chrome, stylized trim, and hood ornaments.

Inside the diners, chrome joined stainless steel for various uses. For seating, an inexpensive vinyl called Naugahyde (just like the kind used in cars) covered both the bench seats and stools. Expensive marble and real stone were on their way out and were replaced by cheap, mass-produced, materials. Stainless steel reigned supreme, however, and took exclusive control of the exterior, giving the diner the appearance of enduring permanence and a feeling of cleanliness. Diner makers promoted the virtues of the "vermin-free" buildings, and restaurateurs paid attention.

Some of the more striking diners assumed a new character with crests made up with neon elements—copying the effect of the fancy hood

TOPS DINER POSTCARD

Hailing from Johnstown, Pennsylvania, Topps Diner featured a full basement (with glass block windows) and an attachéd building in back. This gleaming 1948 vintage Fodero attracted even more attention with the addition of colorful rooftop neon signs, something that most diner owners installed during the early 1950s and 1960s. By that time, the modern convenience known as air conditioning was becoming a standard. *Courtesy Brian Butko*

TOPS DINER — One of Pennsylvania's Finest
Johnstown, Pa.

Tops
DINER
Air Conditioned

THE MODERN HOME CAFE

When the diners vacated the streets of Providence, Rhode Island, many became full-service restaurants. With its distinctive architecture, the Home Cafe is a good example of how to take a diner from the street, fit it into an urban setting, and still retain some classy styling. This Streamline Moderne dream was once located at Middle and Eddy Street in Providence, Rhode Island. *Rhode Island Historical Society. All rights reserved*

ornaments seen on cars. As the competition to capture the customer attention reached a fever pitch, diner owners followed motels, gas stations, and other roadside businesses (including drive-in stands) in the use of elaborate lighting systems. Neon tubing played a major part in this, and by the end of the 1940s sign men bedecked many a diner with a kaleidoscope of color.

As its popularity grew, neon lighting gained widespread acceptance as part of the architecture and design scheme. Instead of using paint or colored porcelain panels, it was the glowing rays of light that bathed the exterior of the all-stainless steel restaurant. To the delight of customers speeding by, colorful tubes of swirling plasma became an electrified welcome mat and turned diners into energetic, roadside beacons. The signal to travelers: Good food and friendly service awaits.

Neon wasn't the only visual trick that diner makers employed. By the mid-1950s, many diners

reached the outer envelope of visual hyperbole. The Paramount Zenith model incorporated a distinctive "wedding cake" design into its corners (complete with a reflecting ball at the top). Fodero gained a following with a stainless steel winged clock above the prep area. Mountain View stole the show with the "cowcatcher," a curved glass and pointed sheet metal combination that made the corners of their diners unique. Even the basic layout was no longer sacred: Doors shifted to the corner, awnings appeared over windows, and vestibules popped out.

With all of these great-looking (and sometimes not-so-great) additions, domestic diner manufacturers transformed the fragile-looking lunch cart into a heavy-duty building. As rock-and-roll music took over the radio airwaves, the diner took its rightful place as a solid, stout symbol of American enterprise.

As it happened, the postwar changes seen on the exterior of diners signaled the beginning of

new things for diners inside—the most important being the addition of women to the workforce. The change of gender (behind the counter) began when most able-bodied men went overseas to fight. Left behind to run things, America's women stepped forward to fill the duties. While legendary gals the likes of "Rosie the Riveter" gained respect on the aircraft assembly lines, women like "Mabel the waitress" earned their own sort of reputation by serving up food and coffee.

The waitress quickly became a diner fixture with more visibility than the cook. She was the interface between the customer and owner, goodwill ambassador, and salesperson. She made it happen,

THE DAUPHIN DREAM

Documented on film during the early years of the 1970s—the decade when the diner was regarded as the Rodney Dangerfield of the restaurant industry—Dauphin's Superior Diner got all the respect it needed from the regular working-class customers in Rochester, New York. At one time, Rochester had 11 Sterling diners, a model made by J. B. Judkins that was constructed in "sliced bread," modular segments. This unit was demolished. *Pedar Ness ©1999*

ZEP DINER MATCHBOOK

During the teens and 1920s, aviation was a growing fascination in America. Because it was so new and novel, anything related to flight could be used for the promotion of goods and services. On the West Coast, gas stations were built in the form of airplanes and diners in the shape of a zeppelin. Located at 15 Florence Avenue in Los Angeles, the Zep Diner was an outfit that stayed "Open All Night." *Preziosi Postcards*

and if you had a good, friendly waitress who liked to make customers happy, a diner visit was like nothing else. On the other hand, if she was a smart-aleck girl like "kiss my grits" Flo (Polly Holliday in the 1970s TV show *Alice*), ordering a simple bowl of chili could prove to be a difficult undertaking at best.

Despite the occasional bad apple, the diner waitress gained notoriety for her matter-of-fact demeanor and willingness to please. As part of diner culture, she evolved into a caricature, an authentic icon of America, often defined by a pink service dress, white shoes, cat's-eye glasses on a chain, a wad of clicking chewing gum, and a big hairdo piled high. She was always ready to take your order, a pad and pen clutched in her hands.

While the diner was a great place to eat before the arrival of the waitress, it became something much more after she hired on. Now diners attained their personality by way of the waitress. Unsung heroes of the restaurant world, diner waitresses worked and continue to work at their respective posts for years, spending their entire lives serving regular customers and those who were just passing through. Ask any inveterate diner owner and they will have a good story to tell about their favorite hand.

As waitresses became a solid diner fixture, a new mode of communication developed between cook and server. Copying the banter that first originated with America's soda jerks, cryptic references became the basis for a new diner slang. A simple order like sausages and mashed potatoes became "Zeppelins in a fog," while an ordinary beef stew became known as "mully" (referring to Mulligan's stew, a favorite hobo road recipe). Even condiments received a new moniker. Butter changed into "skid grease," syrup became "machine oil," and mustard turned into "Mississippi mud." Depending on the town and region, phrases and words varied.

Meanwhile, New Jersey continued in its growing tradition of becoming the American Mecca of diner construction. In 1947, a company that called itself Master Diners started to assemble prebuilt diners in Pequannock. The Manno Dining Car Company followed in 1949 when it opened a shop in the town of Fairfield. With so much competition coming into the local market, the Paterson Vehicle Company (located in Paterson, New Jersey) decided to get aggressive with its national advertising campaign.

During the early 1950s, Paterson touted its Silk City line of diners in industry magazines and printed promotional pieces with particular fervor. One of the more memorable examples featured

FOUNTAIN·DRIVE-IN CANTEEN

COFFEE SHOP · DINING ROOMS

AIRWAYDINER

THE DINER

COFFEE SHOP

PATIO

CLASSIC NEON DINER CLOCK
Along with other roadside businesses of the 1930s and 1940s, diners often featured neon-trimmed timepieces. Some were used to advertise products such as cigarettes, others were merely decorative. Fodero went one step further and used the clock as an integral part of its design scheme. *Shellee Graham @1999*

STREAMLINED AIRWAY DINER
The Boggs Brothers Canteen featured both a drive-in and a diner. It operated during the 1930s and 1940s and was located on U.S. 101 north of San Diego, California. The diner is part of an actual passenger train that ran between San Diego and Old Mexico, many, many years ago. With this eatery, there is no denying the train and diner connection. *Coolstock ©1999*

CHIEF DINER

The Chief Diners were a series of California coffee shops (circa 1980) that took their architectural cues from the school of Streamline Moderne. They were homemade units, outfitted with glass brick accents at the entryway, immense picture windows, a white stucco exterior, and a cool stylized neon sign of an Indian Chief (this was the decade before the onset of what we know now as political correctness). *Dave Wallen ©1999/Courtesy Kent Bash*

average diner man John Macaluso of Clifton, New Jersey. He was living the high life, proof that the diner business could be a lucrative trade and one that provided for a growing family.

Starting in a rundown, five-stool, short order place, Macaluso sold 5-cent hamburgers and saved up enough money to get started in a Silk City unit. The company's handy financing made it easy for him to get into the business and pay off the purchase price, even as the diner supported his lifestyle. The promotional text was explicit: Macaluso earned more than enough money to pay for a new nine-room bungalow with a huge garden and a pair of new automobiles—one of which was a custom-built convertible. (In the ad, a photograph showed the big house and Macaluso at the wheel of his fancy car, a cigar hanging from his mouth.) Most important, the diner income allowed him to raise six children. As the literature

noted, anyone could duplicate this prosperity "with no previous restaurant experience and no dietitian's training."

While some of this ad copy may have been overstated, it was fundamentally true. Back in those days, owning a diner was one type of business that anyone could break into, regardless of their education. Opening a small eatery was a practical plan that allowed the average person (even one lacking any formal schooling or college) to jump up and grab hold of the brass ring.

The modest down payment that the diner maker required to get started in the business was far less than the amount needed to open a garage, hotel, or other high-turnover business. If one takes into consideration the buying power of the dollar 50 years ago and does the math, it's easy to see that opening a diner took a minimal investment in relation to the potential profit.

Irrespective of class, education, or income, the act of opening a diner allowed entry into a special group. Whether it served patrons in New England, the deep South, middle America, the Southwest, or even hundreds of miles west of the Rockies, the American diner business was like a big club. When you bought one, you gained access to a much larger franchise, even though your diner was your own. While food and service varied from location to location, customers could look upon a diner in a new town as being pretty much like their favorite diner at home.

In the years before fast food, it was a great way to do business: A diner owner could individualize his operation and still have wide appeal. No corporate office dictated policy or specified what to serve and how to serve it. The diner owner decided when to open, how much to pay the staff, what foods to put on special, how to advertise, and what the menu should look like. All facets of the operation were in the hands of the owner, and he or she made all the decisions. By combining hard work and imagination, anyone could propel theirs to higher profitability.

With all the diner decisions up to individuals and not corporate think-tanks, there was enough room to act on ideas fast and to do a lot of experimenting. During the 1930s, one of the tastiest of diner ideas got its start after dishware suppliers began making partitioned, blue-colored plates. Diner men saw the possibilities and used the divided platters to serve economical, full meals that they sold at rock-bottom prices. This was the birth of the famed "blue-plate special," a diner standard that endures in many establishments today.

Individual control allowed diners the freedom to serve an eclectic variety too. During the golden age of the diner, regional specialties prevailed and food selection often varied greatly according to the location. During this tasty time, specific diners became known for their unique selection of entrees, appetizers, dinners, drinks, and desserts.

THE FAMILY TAKES A MEAL
The diner was always an equal opportunity restaurant. Everyone and anyone was welcome there, including the family cat and dog. Here, Charles A. Bassett and wife are seen in a 1950s diner (located in Rhode Island) taking a meal with the entire family. It makes you wonder if the pets had their own favorite song on the jukebox. *Rhode Island Historical Society. All rights reserved.*

JERRY O'MAHONY ADVERTISEMENT
The goal of the Jerry O'Mahony Company was to make your diner the "Highest Star." During its peak years of operation, the company touted its quality line of prefabricated restaurants as "the finest diner that money can buy." O'Mahony had a big presence and was a frequent advertiser in industry magazines like *The Diner.* This was the company to propagate the memorable sales slogan, "In our Line we Lead the World." *Preziosi Postcards*

The Diner R=34 Sandwich - Illinois

WRIGHT'S DINER

Wright's Diner (located somewhere along Illinois Route 34) appears to have started out as a small cafe (see the small building, left). It seems the owners were so impressed with train cars that they attached a long, locomotive-type appendage to their small burger shack. With a streamlined end, portholes, and a banner reading "Diner," this outlandish building was both a caricature of the diner and the rail car. *Preziosi Postcards*

Whether you wanted a cut of T-bone steak, a slab of meatloaf, or an "open happy waitress" (an open-faced turkey sandwich that's smothered with gravy), there was sure to be a diner nearby with the menu to suit your taste buds. By the end of the 1950s, many of the large, established diners served up a smorgasbord of food, preparing the meals always in demand, around the clock.

This menu expansion was great for drawing the crowds, but somewhat of a problem for owners. No longer was it enough to have a short-order man who fried by the seat of his pants. The serious diner operator had to hire a cook—sometimes a chef—who knew how to make many foods. In light of spiraling prices and competition from new food operations, remaining profitable dictated a more-rigid protocol for food storage, preparation, and cooking. Wasted stock, wasted time, and wasted effort were costly.

As new food technologies appeared during the late 1950s, some operators saw the convenience of

frozen foods as their salvation, both in the area of meats and vegetables. Influenced by a barrage of industry ads hawking new and improved products (many enhanced with strange new chemicals), some diner owners switched from the tried-and-true to the new. Articles in *The Diner* gave advice on how to best cook the cheaper cuts of meat. Instant ingredients were gaining a foothold in the diner kitchen and, in many people's opinion, setting a bad precedent for the entire industry.

For the time being, customers were oblivious to the gradual changes, as the diner still provided the fun and entertainment they desired. With plenty of quick food, a jukebox selector mounted in every booth (and at regular intervals on the counter), the diner continued to offer a friendly atmosphere that catered to both the blue- and white-collar patrons. For breakfast, lunch, and dinner, the diner remained the daytime and late-night crowd-pleaser well into the late 1950s and early 1960s.

In defiance of the unorthodox, fast-food–style stands that began to appear along the roadways, many diners built a legend for themselves simply by remaining open 24 hours a day (especially in large cities that never seemed to sleep). Those who doubt the after-hours appeal of the diner need only take a gander at artist Edward Hopper's famous painting *Nighthawks*. Before long, they, too, will be down at the local diner—sipping a cup of coffee during those lonely hours after midnight.

With closing time not even a factor, diners had a leg up on most of the emerging burger bars and full-service restaurants. With characteristics unique to its breed, the diner defended its position as a haven for nighthawks, insomniacs, and every other lonely soul who craved human contact during the wee hours.

Nurtured by this nocturnal realm, a palpable diner counter-culture rose up, a tribe of kindred spirits who followed an unwritten code of behavior. Some rules were evident only to the cognoscenti, while the rest were obvious. For instance, if you were dining by yourself and wanted to get a good look at the goings on, you sat at the counter (truck drivers, cabbies, and car-related service people sat here without exception). Dating couples and groups of friends almost always took the booth seats.

There were other established customs, including how to treat your waitress, how best to order food, what not to order, how much to tip, when it was all right to crank up the jukebox volume, and when it was ill-advised to make trouble with other customers. Depending on the diner and the people who owned it, there were certain things that a visitor didn't do—especially when it came to putting down the quality of food in the presence of a proud cook or sensitive waitress. Engaging in the wrong behavior could get you banned for life from your favorite hash house.

But even for the uninitiated who never before set foot inside a prefabricated eatery, diners were a great place to hang out. If a customer sat down and sipped at his coffee long enough, something interesting was always bound to happen. More important, everything that a person needed—including all the modern conveniences—were nearby.

INTERIOR OF SICLIANO'S DINER
This 1946 Silk City diner was formerly run as the Greenville Diner in Greenville, New York. Previously operated by the Sicliano family (this photo was taken just after their purchase during the 1940s), it was recently bought by diner restorer Al Sloan and transported to Alpena, Michigan, to be refurbished. *Courtesy of Al Sloan*

MODERN SNACK BAR SIGN
The Modern Snack Bar is located on Route 25 in Aquebogue, New York (Long Island). This grand neon and bulb sparkler has been in use for more than 35 years. *Courtesy of Larry Schulz*

In the corner, every diner worth its salt had a public pay telephone for making calls to one's wife, bookie, or boss. There was always a clock overhead, allowing those without a watch to know when it was time to hit the road. Of course, there were indoor conveniences, including a toilet, sink, and mirror to check appearance (rest rooms were a haven unto themselves and were kept clean in those days). Only a three-bedroom Cape Cod had more comfort.

Yes, many admirers of the genre view the time spanning from the early 1930s to the late 1950s as the Golden Age of the American diner. Throughout these 30 years, the diner dominated the roadside restaurant trade. It also commanded a place of prominence in the public eye, as it was the diner that came to mind when regular folks thought about eating out, social interaction, and owning their very own business.

Hungry for food, drink, success, entertainment, recreation, escape, camaraderie, friendship, love, relaxation, excitement, music, work, and the company of others, John and Jane America (and their children) took their spot on a stool and looked longingly over the counter for an economical dinner, a generous slice of pie, and a hot cup of Joe (or flagon of ice-cold Coca-Cola). This was the best of times for the diner and an age that would go down in culinary history as the tastiest time for all Americans to eat.

DINER NEON SIGN

Worcester, Massachusetts, is a town rich with diner history. This classic neon beauty still pulls in customers for the Boulevard Diner, a local restaurant fixture and favorite hangout for diner aficionados. Using only the word "Diner" as the description and drawing card, it follows one of the important creeds of the American diner owner: "Keep it simple." *Coolstock ©1999*

CHAPTER FOUR

THE RISE OF AMERICAN ROADFOOD

Hard Times Along the Diner Highways

"Basically this picture represents everything that is good about the Dining Car business. The counterman is in uniform—a clean uniform with a clean cap and a neat little bow tie. He is giving service with a smile in a Diner which shines from its recent cleaning. The counter glistens; the napkin holder and the hood over the back bar have a shine to them; the salad cover is bright and sparkling, not smeared or blurred. Just visible in the background is a neat display case featuring breakfast cereals. The principle of friendly service and cleanliness is the foundation on which the dining car business was built. It doesn't matter whether your car is new or old. With a little extra effort, you can keep it clean; you can certainly see that your countermen or waitresses are dressed in a uniform representative of the food servicing industry. No matter how good your help, they look like a bunch of sloppy 'bohunks' when they stand back of the counter with sleeves rolled up, with no ties and no hats."

The Diner, Volume Three, Number Five, 1946

In 1958, Steve McQueen battled a shapeless alien in the low-budget horror flick *The Blob*. Producers shot the movie at studios in Valley Forge, Pennsylvania, and released it to the drive-ins on a double bill with *I Married a Monster From Outer Space*, another cheesy thriller. Interesting to diner patrons watching in the audience was *The Blob*'s final scene, shot at the real-life Downingtown Diner, a classic Silk City. Horrified that their local eatery was being eaten, Pennsylvanians no doubt perched on the edge of their seats.

In the final scenes of the film, teenage hero McQueen and his girlfriend (along with her pesky little brother) become trapped in the basement of the Downingtown while the blob engulfs the building. Firefighters try to electrocute the alien with high-voltage doses of electricity, but the diner catches fire. Just when it begins to look as if there won't be any dessert for anyone, the hero realizes that the ugly mass hates the cold. McQueen wields a CO_2 fire extinguisher to beat back the monster, buying time until his rescuers round up all the available extinguishers.

Local teens then douse the red menace until they freeze it into a giant pile of intergalactic Jell-O. The military takes over and ships the blob to Antarctica, where it's dropped off by parachute and kept on ice. The Downingtown Diner survives!

Unfortunately, many of the Downingtown's real-life diner compatriots didn't fare so well. By the start of the 1960s, there were a little more than 5,000 diners operating in the country and almost every one began to sense the encroachment of a sinister invader known as competition. As improved roadways and superhighway corridors sliced

THE BEL-BREE DINER
During the 1940s, the Kansas-based building manufacturer known as Valentine Diners made a unit called the Double Deluxe. This diner was larger than the company's smaller eateries and afforded operators more room and more seating for customers. The angled pylon mounted at the front facade was a signature of the line. This Bel-Bree was located in Venice, Florida. It changed identity and became Uncle B's Coney Dogs in 1995. *Marty Lineen Jr. ©1999*

TUMBLE INN DINER

In 1973, Claremont, New Hampshire's Tumble Inn Diner was up for sale. Today, this attractive 1941 Worcester continues to recruit new converts at 1 Main Street. Note the residence next door. In many New England towns, diners could often be found side by side with homes in the urban setting. *Pedar Ness ©1999*

America asunder, a variety of flexible dining formats gained prominence on the roadside.

Coffee shops, cafeterias, hot dog stands, burger huts, pizzerias, family-style eateries, ice cream counters, drive-in restaurants—you name it—they crowded for space along the expanded commercial corridors. Everything imaginable

spilled from this horn of plenty, and all at once, a diversity of dining styles beckoned motorists to "pull over and eat." Why not try something new? Before too long, diner owners saw their established business base threatened and their clientele snatched away.

It would be unfair to suggest that America's diners were caught sleeping at the grill, however. The roadfood invasion wasn't a big secret: It all began in 1908 with the slow, steady sputter of a Model T Ford and by the 1920s swelled into a deafening roar. At the start of the decade, more than eight million passenger vehicles asserted their dominance in the streets.

In 1921, the diner and restaurant industry reached an important crossroads in the battle for the motorist's buck when Jessie G. Kirby commented to a would-be investor that "People in cars are so lazy they don't even want to get out of them to eat!" This ironic statement marked the beginning of a new style of eatery called the Texas Pig Stands and a revolutionary form of automotive dining known as the "drive-in." Almost overnight, speedy service, attentive carhops, and convenience became the roadside features to beat. Diner owners were watching.

SUPERDAWG DRIVE-IN

By the 1970s, drive-in restaurants like the Superdawg Drive-In at Milwaukee and Devon Avenues in Chicago had infiltrated the restaurant market and stolen much of the diner's business. Nevertheless, even the drive-in diners started to fall from grace. Consumers substituted meals eaten in the front seat (while parked) with meals gobbled right at the wheel (while driving). *Howard Ande ©1999*

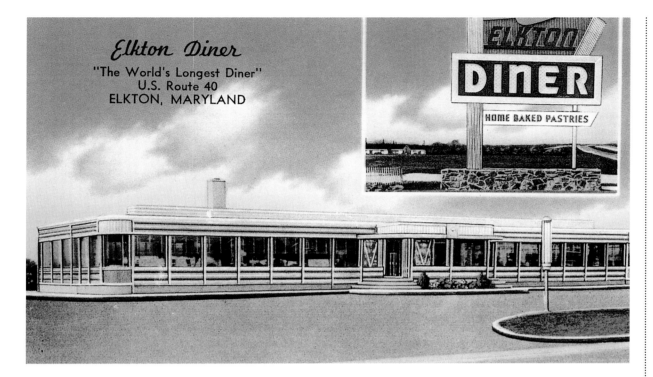

Elkton Diner
"The World's Longest Diner"
U.S. Route 40
ELKTON, MARYLAND

ELKTON
DINER
HOME BAKED PASTRIES

With "curb service" as the trade called it, customers didn't have to park their pride and joy in a lot, leave it unattended, and enter a diner to grab a blue-plate special. As difficult as it was for diner devotees to swallow, the basic premise for dining in diners became the biggest weakness.

Now if a vehicle owner became hungry, he or she could take a break at a handy pit stop where motorists could order food—right from the front seat of their car! Best of all, car customers were able to consume this "new motor lunch" right behind the steering wheel. It was fast, fun, and best of all, hassle free. The interior of the family flivver was now a self-contained dining booth, the dashboard a countertop for laying out the food.

Much to the dismay of dyed-in-the-wool diner men (there were few women owners back then), this revamped style that called for minimized dining facilities captured the attention of the industry. With the success of the Pig Stands in Dallas, Texas, and the famous "Pig Sandwich," a legion of car-serving copycats followed. In spite of the fact that many of the diner manufacturers sold their diners with financing, opening a drive-in was a much more cost-effective option. If a prospective restaurateur considered the final loan payout, freight charges, and expense of interior seating and equipment, diners didn't look so attractive. Operators out to make a fast buck in the restaurant biz found it a whole lot easier to slap together a temporary wooden stand, throw up some overhead canopies, and hire a bevy of beautiful carhops.

THE DOGGIE DINER
Once a part of a small San Francisco diner chain, the Doggie Diner in Alameda, California, was a bold attempt to take back some of the attention the big burger joints had won. During the 1970s, people still had a portion of their stomachs reserved for the types of foods that were served at kitsch mom-and-pop restaurants with zany names and funky architectural themes. *Pedar Ness ©1999*

THE DINER

Unfortunately, many American diners were unable to withstand the fast-food invasion. This O'Mahony diner in Milford, Connecticut, ceased operations in 1978 and alerted former customers with an "Out to Lunch" sign in the front vestibule window. It's gone now and has ended up in the state of Vermont. *Pedar Ness ©1999*

In the carhop department, the best American drive-ins quickly emerged as the roadside shows of the motoring age. This flash-and-sass was more bad news for Diner Joe, since it was nearly impossible to compete with all of those satin-clad gals gliding around on roller skates. How could the ordinary,

workaday diner waitress compare to these parking lot showgirls?

At the biggest drive-ins like the Sivils' famous operation in Dallas, Texas, it was the curb girl who was the main attraction. Dressed in a satin, form-fitting majorette outfit that accentuated all her natural wonders, the serving girl raised the bar of waitressing to a racy new level. In 1940, *Life* magazine summed up the sex appeal of drive-in dining with the catchy headline: "Houston Drive-In Trade Gets Girl Show with Its Hamburgers." Americans were taking notice of the publicity and showed their interest with open wallets and purses.

At the Sivils Drive-Inn, the curb-girls actually put on a live show in the parking lot! At the change of each work shift, servers who left their assigned posts for the day filed into the building as a new team of curb girls made their debut. As music blared out from the loudspeakers, the gals fanned out like dancers in a Busby Berkeley musical. At each side of the parking lot, they lined up in glimmering rows where the persnickety Mrs. Sivils personally inspected them. When everything checked out, she released the gals to serve the customers in their cars.

CHIEF DINER

Out on the San Fernando Road in San Fernando, California, the Chief Diner stood alone as a California diner. Because of its location and uniqueness, it managed to eke out an existence among the many fast-food restaurants along the strip. *Pedar Ness ©1999*

Valentine

MANUFACTURING, INC.

POST OFFICE BOX 667

WICHITA, KANSAS

The LITTLE CHEF

As if these sort of antics weren't enough to seduce diner fans, drive-in restaurants employed even more outlandish tactics to woo customers. Some added small movie screens atop service buildings and showed cartoons and other short reels. Many featured scantily clad cigarette girls who wheeled around the lots on scooters. A few piped popular music into the parking lot. One operator in the South even provided car air-conditioning gadgets (patrons stuffed a large tube into the vent window for cold air). It appeared that there was no end to the drive-in novelty.

With all of the glamour and excitement that the drive-in eateries promised, the number of car service outfits with carhops eventually outnumbered the

boxy diners with inside stools and serving counters. By the mid-1960s, there were more than 26,000 drive-ins operating in the United States with more waitresses strapping on a pair of roller skates every day.

To repel the aggressive advance of these competing restaurants, diner owners called in the cavalry as best they could. In the beginning, a few slipshod managers concluded that if they just tacked on curb service as yet another diner "feature," the lost customers would return. In theory, it was a great idea, but it was like trying to make a Ford into a Duesenberg by altering the body.

Because of basic floor plan considerations and the general arrangement of entries and exits, most of the existing premanufactured eateries were ill-

HI WAY DINER

Claiming to make the "Best Hot Dog in Arizona," Chaunce's Hi Way Diner is a vintage Valentine unit. Built in Wichita, Kansas, the Valentines were self-contained structures and transported by rail to all points. This one is located in Flagstaff, Arizona. *Pedar Ness ©1999*

MAX'S GRILL

Max's Grill in Harrison, New Jersey, is another survivor. A 1920s Kullman, it's one of those barrel-roofed, quaint little buildings evocative of the early diner designs. Constructed before the stainless steel period of the 1950s and 1960s, it managed to carve out a niche for itself as the burger wars raged on. Today, it's still a favorite neighborhood bodega. *Ronald Saari ©1999*

suited for attending to people who liked to dine in the parking lot. To make outside service more practical, some diner men tried to circumvent their building's breeding by modifying their diner's architecture. The DeRaffele Company took this concept to heart and debuted a factory-built unit with an overhead canopy and a walk-up service window. (Industry stalwarts could not believe their eyes.)

More often than not, diners remained diners and made due with what they had. As a stop-gap effort, those without the cash to remodel simply threw up a sign that read "Carhop Service" and then instructed their team of reluctant waitresses to march out and take food orders from customers in the parking lot.

The White Castle Hamburgers chain (and also the White Towers chain, their imitator) of hamburger bars was one of the most visible examples in this regard. Early in the roadfood game, White Castle used its everyday waitresses to take care of the cars at the curb. During their heyday, many Castles operated in urban areas where there wasn't any parking to begin with, so the idea of serving cars that queued up streetside meshed well with the existing format. (Later, these porcelain-clad eateries made the drive-up service window a part of the building.)

Nevertheless, White Castle was the exception to the rule and in the end, the unholy marriage of the drive-in restaurant and the diner didn't last. Like oil and vinegar, the two formats repelled each other and remained in their own distinct domains.

There were some other solutions for the diner industry to consider and a few of the manufacturers presented acceptable answers. In 1949, Paramount

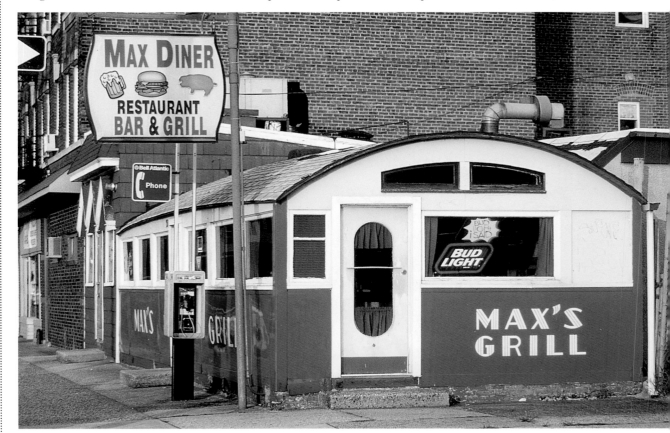

Diners acknowledged the drive-in pressure on the diner business when it introduced a double-duty diner model called the "Roadking." Taking on the size and appearance of a modest travel trailer, this new beauty was factory designed to handle both "diner and road stand business" at the same time. Unlike most normal diners, it possessed all the extra features that allowed for all three possibilities: parking lot curb service, walk-up clientele, and of course, inside seating (although the lack of space severely limited comfort).

Encased in glorious bands of decorative stainless steel, the King featured a well-positioned pass-through window where the carhops could pick up the food order without ever going inside. Outfitted with this regal diner, a few happy Pappies held their own among the drive-ins and even made some good money. One satisfied owner reported doing more than $300 a day on short-order business alone—a respectable volume for the time.

In 1938, an upstart company called Valentine Manufacturing began making a line of highly portable diners designed to address the fast-paced road stand trade. Over a 36-year span, founder Arthur Valentine turned his vision of building affordable diners into reality by designing a practical line of "portable steel sandwich shops." Before

LARRY'S DINER SIGN
Larry's unforgettable coffee cup diner sign was a favorite sight in Fairfield, Connecticut, circa 1975. Within the last 10 years, Larry's was moved from its Route 1 location and became part of a different restaurant (and the sign was lost). There are a lot of diner buffs crying. Soon, this once-complete diner will change hands again and become an Italian restaurant. *Pedar Ness ©1999*

THE DUCHESS DINER
The Duchess Diner was known as a "dineraunt," a combination of a diner and a restaurant. In spite of its modern leanings, this eatery commanded a strong presence after dark—a potent example of how the right lighting can enhance and improve. This diner was located in West Haven, Connecticut, circa 1978. *Pedar Ness ©1999*

ROADSIDE DINER

This canopied and window-curtained marvel gained a measure of fame by appearing in the John Sayles movie, *Baby, It's You*. Located in Wall, New Jersey, it's a 1950s vintage Silk City (built in New Jersey by the Paterson Vehicle Company). *Ronald Saari ©1999*

CARNEY'S TRAIN DINER

Carney's Express Limited is part of a three-restaurant chain in Los Angeles, California. A tried-and-true theme restaurant that plays on the popularity of the diner, this location attracts hungry rail lovers in Studio City, California. *Pedar Ness ©1999*

the company ended operations in 1974, it made a respectable dent in the American diner market with 2,200 units sold.

Valentines were just the ticket for those short-order cooks who wanted to start their own food service enterprise on the roadside. First, they were a lot less costly than most of the large premanufactured diners, and diner setup crews could install them with minimal fuss. Best of all, the little Valentine diner left its factory complete: All of the restaurant fixtures needed to get up and running in the shortest time possible came with the package.

Most prominent in the Valentine models was the small kitchen arrangement, engineered for efficient "assembly-line" operation and outfitted with all the popular amenities, including stainless-steel shelves, sink, and countertops. In the same spirit of the old time Buckley wagons, an externally vented fry station, a combo refrigerator and freezer, and an extremely petite toilet facility completed the well-thought-out, tightly packed diner package. Small-time operators running on a shoestring loved it.

Valentine's most popular diner was a 10-stool model called the "Little Chef," a versatile eatery that featured three floor plans with an inside counter and a convenient walk-up take-out window (all in a compact footprint of 10x25 feet). It sold for a little more than $9,000.

Entrepreneurs with more money could choose the expanded "Double Deluxe," a large model outfitted with seven sit-down booths. Along

RHINEBECK DINER
Route U. S. 9
RHINEBECK, N. Y.

with the stools and counter, this unit offered comfortable seating for 36 patrons. It was as close to a full-sized diner as you could get without visiting New Jersey.

A major advantage to the Valentine diners was their size and weight. With their operations based in Wichita, Kansas (they also maintained a sales office in West Hempstead, New York), the company enjoyed equidistant access to all surrounding states. That was important for spreading the diner gospel nationwide, since the shipping freight added a substantial amount to a diner's final price. (To cover delivery and set-up, the Valentine buyers of the 1960s paid a freight charge of 80 cents for each mile.)

The company routinely used the rail lines for transport. In fact, railroad tracks ran right alongside the manufacturing facilities at 1020 South McComas

Street in Wichita, allowing easy shipment of Valentine units to virtually any point in the country. Valentine loaded one or more of the tiny diners onto rail cars and delivered them to their point of purchase in a matter of days. (From there, a truck hauled them to site.) In places where immense diners never ventured, Valentines paved the way.

Unfortunately, the low cost and ease of delivering the Valentines didn't cause them to overpopulate the roads. In spite of the fact that they looked cozy and were cheap to buy, they had a limited profit potential in relation to the number of seats. The narrow, concentrated approach of the Valentines was still somewhat impotent when compared to the kind of drive-ins that afforded acres of parking and restaurants with every luxury.

RHINEBECK DINER EXTERIOR

New York's Rhinebeck Diner handled the problem of automobiles with simple aplomb: "Park Your Car in the Rear." Located on U.S. 9, the Rhinebeck offered fountain service and a canvas canopy to protect the patrons entering from the street. The only thing missing from this upscale-looking diner restaurant setup was a uniformed doorman. *Courtesy Roger Jackson*

THE MAYFAIR DINER

As diners go, the Mayfair diner is the diner pride and joy of Philadelphia, Pennsylvania. This custom-built, unbelievably long (188 and 1/2 feet) O'Mahony is the Titanic of diners. The menu is just as big. Patrons can sup on hundreds of selections—everything from veal cutlets and shrimp to steaks, chops, fresh fish (never frozen), burgers, and breakfasts. *Ronald Saari ©1999*

A MODERN DINER

The late 1970s was a rather tough time for diners. By then, new models were exhibiting much of the architectural modernism found in some of the West Coast coffee shops. This futuristic diner was located in West Haven, Connecticut. *Pedar Ness ©1999*

The diner industry had to implement bolder plans if it wanted to win back public affection. To regain their respect, diners needed a full-fledged whopper that played off the customer's pride. The timing for this psychological offensive couldn't have been better. During the 1950s, the economic prosperity that painted the postwar decade the color of money caused an obvious expansion in the physical size of just about everything. Automobile bodies ballooned up to exaggerated proportions, homes expanded, and hairdos became more puffed up than they ever were (the towering beehive was a perfect example).

On the shelves of the local supermarket, the "king size" box made its debut. At the same time, bodybuilder Charles Atlas showed skinny boys how huge muscles could bolster their self-esteem. Marilyn Monroe set a buxom example for young girls. In all facets of life, America attempted to outdo the world with its big, brash, bold way of life. As expectations swelled, perceived size became more important than quality.

Capitalizing on this climate for bigger and better things, new diners emerged from the factories, heavily influenced by the oversized ideal. Eatery owners saw bigger profits in the behemoth and embraced the concept. Everywhere the motorist

even profitable—to operate a quaint little eatery that had just a half-dozen booths and a cramped, 10-stool counter.

Nevertheless, the Titanic-style of diner restaurant wasn't the answer for every diner operation. If an owner lacked the additional funds to purchase a brand-new diner, there were less-expensive alternatives to consider for drumming up customer interest. Many decided to enlarge their image by using some good old American showmanship. The imaginative diner men who were waiting in the wings still had a few more tricks up their sleeve.

One shrewd diner man opted for the installation of a half-dozen hobby-horses instead of standard counter stools. With this indoor corral of broncos, he sparked the imagination of the younger crowd and, in the process, influenced parents by way of their children (a common roadside practice).

RED ONION CAFE PLATE LUNCH
Farm Security Administration photographer Russell Lee captured this Crystal City, Texas, scene in 1939. Small-time operations like this would last only a few decades more. After World War II, roads and the nature of travel changed dramatically, and along with it, so did the business of dining out. *Library of Congress*

gazed, diners touted themselves as being the biggest and the best. Neon signs, picture postcards, dinner menus, newspaper ads—wherever diner owners could paint or install the proclamation—giant diners proclaimed their immensity to the American consumer.

The architectural Godzilla tactic worked wonders: By adding the extra seats and stools allowed by the expanded floor space, operators tapped into a viable format for boosting the bottom line. More customers meant more food sales.

Always eager to please, diner manufacturers fueled the growing frenzy for "jumbo-sized" diners. In 1954, the Kullman Dining Car Company lauded itself in industry ads "as being twice selected to build the world's *largest* diner." But the DeRaffele Diner Manufacturing Company didn't play second fiddle in this arena. It countered with its own braggadocio, claiming it built "the world's *longest* diner." As a *Diner* magazine advertisement of the day described it, the DeRaffele model was "longest in size, longest in modern features and longest in profit potential."

No doubt about it, diners were getting larger by the minute and those who purchased them were no longer content to occupy tiny slivers of land. Besides, it was no longer good enough—or

Interestingly enough, it was this basic "let's make the children happy" idea that resurfaced years later as the elaborate fast-food playground.

In Cleveland, diner man Kenny King jumped on the promotional merry-go-round with a novel treasure chest gimmick: As part of his plan, children picked up a special membership card and joined what he called the "clean your plate" club. If the kids shoveled down all of their food, they had the chance to pick out a cheap trinket from the pirate's booty. It was a big hit with the little ones and no one went away empty handed. The toys flowed freely even when the child couldn't finish the large, diner-size portions.

America's diner operators had to be a little more sophisticated when it came to enticing the older set and securing their regular business. While the principles were the same, the main difference to consider

was age. In terms of appealing to one's innate desires, the hook had to draw in mature audiences.

And so, proprietors created a dining environment that exuded escape, calm, and comfort. In a

continued on page 115

PORT SILVER THERMOMETER
Before the age of the corporate oligarchy, diners and other restaurants used to give away useful mementos like thermometers and calendars. This "We Like Children" temperature gauge was given out by the Port Silver diner in Milwaukee, Wisconsin. Today, freebies are limited to Beanie Babies and promotional tie-ins to major motion pictures. *Preziosi Postcards*

WESTERNER DRIVE-INN
The Westerner Drive-Inn serves them in their car on the old cut of Route 66 in Tucumcari, New Mexico. During the 1930s, drive-ins became quite a novelty for the motorist. By the end of the 1950s, they managed to reduce the status of America's diners and to many, looked liked they were taking over. *Howard Ande ©1999*

MEL'S

MEL'S DRIVE-IN
8585 Sunset Boulevard ★ West Hollywood, California

In 1989, California restaurateur Steven Weiss was cruising along Hollywood's Sunset Boulevard when he passed by a particularly interesting restaurant called Ben Frank's. This was no ordinary eatery, but a one-of-a-kind structure that screamed for attention at the top of its lungs. It was built in the style of coffee shop moderne, or "Googie," as the architectural historians called it, after the famous 1950s restaurant that popped out eyeballs along the strip.

With a mischievous gleam in his eye of a man who just saw something that he really wants, Weiss turned to his wife and said, "Now, that would make a great location for a Mels!" Already the proprietor of three American Graffiti–style eateries, he wanted more. Weiss was searching for a flamboyant centerpiece that was worthy of the Mels name.

And what an important name it was: Roadside scholars know that it was Steven's father, the real-life Mel, who first brought the name to the attention of the motoring crowd. Back in 1947, he was the visionary who introduced carhops and curb-service to the California market with his drive-ins on South Van Ness and Geary Streets in San Francisco. It was at the second Mels where son Steven first

cued in on the biz. While in high school, he worked the counter as a soda jerk, serving ice cream and mixing up shakes (and mean banana splits).

Steven continued down the path of serving food to the public and eventually had the wherewithal to resurrect the legendary Mels name (the original site on Van Ness was torn down after George Lucas filmed American Graffiti). Weiss rebuilt the eatery on Lombard Street and charged up the modern version with 1950s style. The retro feel restaurant became a great hit with the public and a short while later, he opened a second diner on Geary Street. He was in the process of establishing a third Mels in Sherman Oaks (an affluent Los Angeles suburb) when his eyes were opened to the possibilities of the Ben Frank's location.

There were good reasons for Weiss' new obsession with real estate along Sunset Strip. Like many West Coast icons, Ben Frank's possessed a rich history. Since 1959, it held prominence as the "in" dining hangout of West Hollywood. Open 24 hours a day, Frank's was a comfortable place where people could relax. The famous, infamous, and ordinary were drawn there to chow down on legendary burgers, sandwiches, and

MELS VINTAGE DRIVE-IN
Made famous in the George Lucas film *American Graffiti,* the Mels Drive-In that was located on San Francisco's South Van Ness was truly the quintessential curb service operation. Today, Steven Weiss continues to operate Mels units throughout California and continues to provide the nostalgic atmosphere of the 1950s to modern-day customers. *Courtesy of Steven Weiss*

MELS SUNSET BOULEVARD

With its exaggerated lines and unconventional design, the so-called "Googies" style of architecture (typical of the vintage Ben Franks) was the perfect match for a Mels drive-in diner. California restaurateur Steven Weiss sought to lease the structure for years and succeeded in 1997. *Pedar Ness ©1999*

pancakes. Celebrities like James Dean and Andy Warhol were regulars. When it came to food, everyone could get what they wanted and even rock-and-roll bands like the Rolling Stones stopped in to eat.

Nevertheless, the transitory nature of Los Angeles had its effect and Ben Frank's eventually fell out of favor with the fashionable crowds. By the 1980s, fast-food stands and drive-through ordering lanes ruled the day and celluloid idols found more exclusive places to haunt. Now, the sit-down stool-and-booth diner was no longer such an attractive place for a power lunch, regardless of how spiffy the terrazzo floor looked or how innovative the building architecture was.

Enter the current owner of the Ben Frank's property, stage left. He figured that a place to serve up food was just fine, but had an idea for a more profitable use of the land. Unfortunately, these plans didn't call for renovation or the dedication of a historical landmark. He wanted to raze the building and replace it with yet another mini-mall.

Suddenly, one of southern California's last remaining Googie-style structures became the center of a hot debate. Before long, the argument engaged the entire town. City officials in West Hollywood vehemently opposed the mini-mall plan and began a campaign to save the historic building.

As outraged patrons and local residents joined the fight, the property changed hands. In 1991, real estate investment partners David Kermani and Barbara Krantz became the new owners. Now, even grander plans were afoot: Instead of building a mall, they would erect a three-story office and retail building. Fans of Ben Frank's were outraged.

One year later, the matter went to court and Kermani won the right to build whatever he wanted. As luck had it, the real estate market slumped and the plans to build the offices were put on hold. That's when city planner Jennifer Davis got involved: She took advantage of the delay and began to "educate" Kermani on the building's historical and architectural significance and why it was such a valuable resource for the city. Meanwhile, Ben Frank's restaurant operation continued unabated, amid all of the controversy. A 1994 vote to have it declared a historical landmark fell short by one vote.

While the fate of Ben Frank's remained in question, new problems surfaced. Suddenly the county health department ordered the restaurant closed and required that it meet modern building codes. Of course, this meant costly renovations for the proprietors. So, when the lease came up for renewal in 1996, they locked the doors forever (or so they thought).

Still, good fortune smiled on the building: Boosters of the 1950s modern structure finally persuaded Kermani to spare it from demolition.

Throughout this period of flux, Steven Weiss tried unsuccessfully to convince the various owners to lease the property to him. Now, after seven years, he was given the opportunity to sign a 20-year lease on his Sunset Boulevard dream location. It was 1997 and the future of the Googie-style time machine looked bright. Weiss planned to restore as much as he could and bring the rest up to modern standards. To make it accessible for disabled patrons, he renovated the rest rooms. At the same time, he added a decidedly Californian twist: an outdoor patio with seating for 50.

A few months later, the old Ben Frank's was reborn as a new Mels. As luck had it, Weiss opened the dining room to coincide with the original drive-in's 50th anniversary. So the next time you're cruising down Sunset, put on your Wayfarers and stop off at that crazy Googie they call Mels. Try the Melburger, Lumpy Mashed Potatoes, or a bowl of Grandma's Chicken Soup. Slurp down a cherry, vanilla, or chocolate Coke, and stock up on napkins. You'll be asking the same question as many transplanted East Coasters: "Who says there aren't any good diners in California?"

DINER JEWELRY

New Mexico artist Harvey Kaplan fuels the feeding frenzy for diner memorabilia with his wonderful creations. He designs and crafts an entire line of "Roadside Jewelry" that's a favorite of modern-day diner fans. *Allen Bryan ©1999/Courtesy of Harvey Kaplan*

TURNABOUT DINER SIGN

In 1976, the shoulders lining New Jersey's Route 22 (this sign was in Phillipsburg) were thick with diners and diner signs. It's ironic that many of these eateries were in the process of going out of business or shutting it down for good, as a turnabout in the business was only a decade away. The great diner renaissance was barreling down the pike. Soon, many of the old, forgotten places would enjoy their revival. *Pedar Ness ©1999*

HITS THE JACKPOT!

The NEW PARAMOUNT "ROADKING"!

Owner
Charles Simonton
Route #8
Blairstown, N. J.

reports:

"Sensational Profits."

Doing over $300.00 per day on strictly short-order business, Mr. Simonton finds the new Paramount Roadking the most sensational profit deal ever.

Set up to handle both diner and roadstand business, the Roadking is your opportunity to get into profitable diner operation for a minimum investment.

Constructed by Paramount, the Roadking incorporates every advantage of Paramount's engineering skill. Material used is exactly the same as used in the custom built Paramount Diners.

Write today for complete information on this revolutionary new diner-restaurant business.

Incidentally, one model available for immediate delivery.

PARAMOUNT DINERS, Inc.

500 Belmont Avenue   Sherwood 2-9025   Haledon 2, N. J.

continued from page 111

foreshadowing of those hackneyed "theme" restaurants of the 1980s, some diners raised the intensity of interior aesthetics. A few installed immense fish tanks or had hand-painted murals applied on their walls. Others decided to take a practical route and add padded furniture. New styles of decor gained in popularity with owners, and diners that were once content to look utilitarian on the inside became an interior decorator's nightmare. In an effort to entertain, diners enrolled the aid of table-top gadgets. Before long, perfume dispensers and fortune-telling boxes found residence in the diner booth. (Remember the classic *Twilight Zone* episode where William Shatner and his girlfriend are held captive by a devilish tabletop device?)

You didn't have to be clairvoyant, however, to see that diners were moving away from their roots. Strange as it was, diners began to hide the simple fact that they were diners and, to their detriment, tried to show the public that they could be just like any other restaurant of the day. This single act may very well have contributed to their decline. Despite all of the interior, exterior, and promotional efforts that owners tried to retake the lead in the roadfood race, the diner format continued to falter.

For good or ill, the future of dining was evolving. The most devastating development had already occurred back in the days of 1937—with hardly anyone taking notice. That fateful year, a new enemy appeared on the radar screen. At first, it was a mere blip. It was the grand opening that signaled the entry of brothers Mac and Maurice

THE BLOB DEVOURS THE DOWNINGTOWN

Starring actor Steve McQueen, *The Blob* featured Pennsylvania's real-life Downingtown Diner. Today, the original movie diner is gone, but a replacement is operating as the Cadillac Diner in the town of Downingtown. *Coolstock ©1999*

THE PARAMOUNT ROADKING

The Roadking was Paramount's answer to the short-order, limited-menu roadside stand business. A self-contained diner, it was small, portable and had the distinct advantage of being able to serve inside customers, walk-up business, and those customers who were arriving in their cars. *Preziosi Postcards*

When compared to self-service gasoline stations, express checkout grocery lanes, and other efficient forms of service, standard carhop service wasn't that fast anymore. On the business side of carhops, there were too many personnel matters to handle. The McDonalds had more than their share of problems with employee turnover and absence due to sickness. The pilfering of food, supplies, and serving utensils was another expensive issue.

At the same time, sloppy practices in the kitchen were a cause for concern. The big variety of menu items restricted the cooks' ability to master any one of them and prepare it with top efficiency. With a large menu of foods, the McDonalds stored a roomful of ingredients on site, increasing the chance of spoilage (something the nation's diner men already knew about).

Convinced that the operation could stand some improvements, the McDonalds closed down the octagonal drive-in at Fourteenth and E Streets for three months. They decided that it was time to

NORM'S COFFEE SHOP

Norm's Coffee Shop highlights the direction that many eateries took out on the West Coast. While a few diners were imported to the Los Angeles, California, region, the architectural style that emerged was "Googies," or exaggerated modern. Out here, cars were king and railroad-car style buildings held little appeal. With the pace of life so fast, sharp angles, dramatic signage, and bold colors were needed to build an audience. *Pedar Ness ©1999*

THE HUB DINER POSTCARD

Billing itself as "The Diner of Counter and Car Service," the Hub Diner of Beaumont, Texas (located on U.S. 90 at the Circle, along College Street), offered the best of both worlds: carhop service and inside seating. As drive-ins increased in popularity during the 1950s and 1960s, many diners were forced to address the format of in-car dining. Nevertheless, organized, double-duty operations like the Hub were a minority. *Preziosi Postcards*

McDonald into the business of roadside food. The pair had opened a refreshment stand in the California city of Arcadia and, like many small-time operators who blazed the trail before them, based their tiny outpost on the drive-in format.

The brothers proceeded to do a great business serving the automobiles traveling along Route 66, and within a few years success inspired them to open an even more ambitious stand. In 1940, they sliced the building they called the Airdrome in two and moved it to a busy street intersection in San Bernardino. There—in a remodeled form—it pulled in a mob of motoring car customers over the next eight years. The blip was now a force of its own and something the restaurant industry would soon acknowledge.

After World War II, the McDonald brothers noticed that the customers in their ever-speedier cars were getting more impatient.

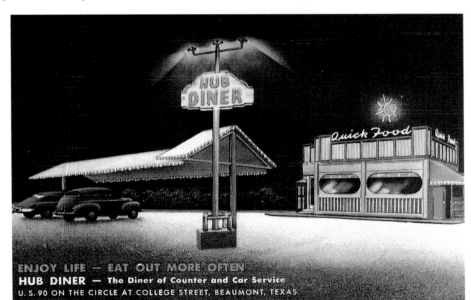

ENJOY LIFE — EAT OUT MORE OFTEN
HUB DINER — The Diner of Counter and Car Service
U.S. 90 ON THE CIRCLE AT COLLEGE STREET, BEAUMONT, TEXAS

reshape the drive-in formula into a new entity—one that operated on speed, efficiency, and self-service. As part of this fine-tuning process, they reduced the menu to nine food items. They also fired the carhops, sacked the dishwasher, and got rid of the dishes and silver (in favor of paper and plastic). They called this new format the "Speedy Service System" and began to promote the assembly-line concept of making and selling hamburgers.

At first, serious restaurateurs took scant notice of the funny little diner wannabe. When the article, "One Million Hamburgers and 160 Tons of French Fries a Year" was first published in the July 1952 issue of the *American Restaurant*, most of the

diners operating nationwide shrugged off the news as a regional fluke. What damage could two California upstarts wreak on a business that was more than 80 years old?

It might go over in California, but what New Englander would want to eat a hamburger sandwich made one way, without exception, that they had to order and pick up themselves at a self-service window? Diners featured comfy booths, spacious counters, and waitresses who answered the customer's beck and call. With good food and service, diners would always have loyal customers.

Overwhelming customer response soon answered the question. Within a year, the concept

CROSS KEYS DINER
Located in New Oxford, Pennsylvania, the Cross Keys Diner was once an air-conditioned haven for car customers. While joining three barrel-roofed diners may have worked during the 1920s, it was no longer an adequate solution by the 1950s. Competing national chain restaurants like Howard Johnson's and Stucky's made their appearance and were being built from the ground up to accommodate huge crowds. *Courtesy of Brian Butko*

Cross Keys Diner
NEW OXFORD, PA.

eateries only had one of the multispindle mixers). When he saw the long lines and the customer enthusiasm, he struck up a deal to duplicate the idea and take it to America.

The resulting plan to franchise the Speedy Service System was a runaway hit. By 1959, the juggernaut reached terminal velocity when Kroc opened more than 100 of the new McDonald's walk-up stands. With more on the way, he was selling hamburgers, French fries, and milkshakes like no ordinary diner before him could sell any type of food.

Now the diner industry was watching—in horror. Along with every other type of roadside restaurant, they were in big-time trouble. There was nothing that the diners could do to stop progress. Like a Tsunami, the fast-food hamburger stand clones rolled across America. Using the business format proven by the McDonald brothers, returning servicemen eager to get into the business of roadside food gained their own market foothold.

Years later, as our young men left home to fight in Vietnam, towering marquees blocked the motorist's view of the few classic diners that remained. New players with names like Carrol's, Carter's, Biff's, Burger Chef, Burger King, Golden Point, Hardee's, Jiffy, Kelly's, Mr. Fifteen, Sandy's,

AL MAC'S DINER

At 135 President Avenue, Al Mac's diner continues to be the toast of Fall River, Massachusetts. Here is a resplendent DeRaffele diner, manufactured in 1953. The current diner is one of a string that diner man Al McDermott owned. Eight years ago, it faced possible demolition but was saved. At that time, it was lifted off its foundation and moved to face west while the rotting neon sign was rebuilt. Who said there are no happy diner endings? *Ronald Saari ©1999*

took root and scores of competitors were duplicating the McDonalds' plan. A few years later, Ray Kroc, a salesman for the Prince Castle company, traveled by car to the McDonalds' stand to see why they needed 10 heavy-duty Multimixers (most

ZINN'S DINER

Still operating today, Zinn's Diner continues as a Pennsylvania roadside landmark. With its "Pennsylvania Dutch"–style of home cooking, Zinn's is living proof that individually owned diners can still attract a loyal clientele by concentrating on the quality of food. Of course, it doesn't hurt to have a large statue positioned out in front. *Courtesy of Brian Butko*

Steer-In, and Wetson's stole the motorist's attention away from the diners. For the average consumer, the view through the windshield became more complicated, more cluttered, and even more confusing.

To make matters worse, the ever-dwindling attention span of the motorist promised to get even shorter. The year 1956 marked a turning point in America's mobility when Congress approved the Interstate Highway Program. The implications were substantial for all forms of roadside commerce, since the long-range plans called for 40,000 miles of widened, four-lane routes that would link together 90 percent of major U.S. cities.

These 26,500 interstate miles were to be constructed by the close of the 1960s. The rest of the high-speed roads were to follow soon after. In the wake of these new superhighways—with their business-choking bypass routes taking motorists around, not through, cities, their predetermined rest stops, and restricted access ramps—diners had

to rewrite every known rule of roadside food, one more time. Diners were in for more hard times.

Roadside restaurants had 10 years to get their house in order and to formulate a counter-offensive. Unfortunately, the battle was almost as futile as the fighting in the Far East. As early as the mid-1960s, many of the gloomy forecasts that critics made for the restaurant industry became a reality. For America's remaining diner owners, the statistics were frightening: Out of the 378,460 restaurants that were doing business that year, 215,080—more than half—fell in the fast-food category.

Now, Americans were in more of a hurry to go somewhere else. No longer was the activity of eating on the road viewed as such a special activity. Motorists were dizzy with high-speed highways and the ability to travel long distances without stopping.

Once accustomed to this accelerated clip of living, many found it uncomfortable to stop and languish in what they perceived were excruciatingly

O'ROURKE'S DINER
Middletown, Connecticut, is where the motorist will find the eatery known as O'Rourke's. This vintage 1946 Mountain View features a great neon sign. Those locals who like real diner food ignore all of the other restaurant placards along Main Street and reserve their loving gaze for O'Rourke's. Inside, 15 counterside stools and 6 booths take a daily workout. *Coolstock ©1999*

BECOME *the* FAVORITE IN TOWN

with a SILK CITY DINER

Old friends and old songs may be best, but old Diners cost you money. Replacement with the new SILK CITY DINER means complete modernization at the lowest possible cost, and gives you the opportunity to own "The most popular spot in town." The SILK CITY DINER comes complete with kitchen, lavatories, dishes and cooking utensils. All back bar fixtures are of stainless steel. Walls, floor and counter are finished in colorful tiles. New improved lighting and ventilation. The patented construction of this steel car offers many advantages found only in SILK CITY DINER. Investigate now.

The SILK CITY is the biggest quality Diner ever priced so low. But our liberal trade-in allowance makes it a still greater value. Compare for yourself —let us estimate the trade-in value of your old Diner *today*.

FOUR YEARS TO PAY

SILK CITY is qualified to offer you a sounder and more liberal payment plan than ever before. There are no hidden strings—our 4-year payment plan is designed to make things as easy as possible for you to "pay out of profits." Let us give you the details. No obligation.

SILK CITY DINERS

MANUFACTURED BY PATERSON VEHICLE COMPANY
EAST 27TH STREET AND 19TH AVENUE
PATERSON, N. J.
ESTABLISHED 1906

SILK CITY DINERS 'FAVORITE' AD

The Paterson Vehicle Company (located in Paterson, New Jersey) was aggressive with its national advertising campaign. During the early 1950s, Paterson touted its Silk City line of diners in industry magazines and printed promotional pieces with particular fervor. This ad promoted a liberal pay-out plan for those wishing to finance their diner dreams. *Preziosi Postcards*

slow, pay-when-you-are-finished-eating diners. The endless road—with all the wonders it promised—beckoned. When you took lunch at the fast-food order window, you could remain in your car. It only took a few minutes to pick up food, allowing one to zoom back onto the superslab without slowing down.

By now, Americans were regularly taking their vacations by automobile, and road travel grew to become an industry all by itself. The growing ranks of sight-seers wheeling away to "See the U.S.A. in

their Chevrolet" spawned a variety of restaurants that were eager to cash in on the cross-country trip.

To satiate the station wagon adventurers and to make them feel comfortable while miles away from home, the corporate chain stores got wise to the idea that every one of their outlets should look, feel, taste, and smell the same—regardless of location. This standardization would reduce much of the confusion the customer felt when visiting a strange city for the first time. There—right on the corner—would be the same hamburger stand or chicken shack as the ones in their own hometown.

Part of this duplication plan was to adopt the latest architecture and to keep the buildings and parking lots in immaculate condition. A sagging roof, dirty windows, worn countertops, threadbare floors, peeling paint, or grease stains splattered onto the ceiling were rare in this type of eatery.

Of course, this deep pockets approach created a lot of pressure on the small-town diner men who owned older diners that by now were looking a little worse for wear and tear. Against their will, many diner owners hung their heads in shame and vowed to keep up with appearances. Those who could afford the expensive price of renovation took the "face-lift" route.

This wasn't the type of task for the weekend handyman to try. Only an experienced craftsman could bring a diner back to its day of splendor. The unique elements that make up a typical interior and exterior are not the materials that can be easily reworked with a hammer or beautified with a layer of paint.

Looking to the manufacturer was of little use, since it was best if workers performed restorative work on location. It was unheard of to *detach* a diner and transport it back to the factory for refurbishing. Even if the diner makers offered the service, the costly freight would have made it a moot point. Back in those days, diner doctors were required to make house calls.

In this field, the father-and-son team of Erwin and Erwin Fedkenheuer were the best-known of the diner renovators. As documented by Richard Gutman, the elder Erwin perfected his skills in bending sheet-metal during a 20-year stint at Paramount Diners. In 1956, he got the notion to strike out on his own and enticed two of the company's top metal workers to join him. Along with Erwin Junior as the salesman, they started the Erfed Corporation. High on hope, they intended to build high-quality food service equipment and to "specialize in the repair, modernization and renovation of existing Diners on location."

It was hard work and it wasn't easy to make a silk purse out of a sow's ear—especially if that sow was a homemade diner or old lunch car infested with termites. Still, the Erfed team worked many miracles on decrepit night owls and routinely worked their magic while the diner remained open. As the customers dined in one half of the structure, the Erfred elves worked diligently nearby, redoing worn floor tiles, installing windowsills, nailing down loose moldings, and resurfacing countertops and tables with fresh layers of the new Formica.

Along with interior remodeling, the typical diner renovation assignment may have called for upgrading a dated, railroad-style monitor roof with a more modern, linear parapet. Enlarging the windows yielded dramatic results on some of the early

POLAR BEAR FROZEN CUSTARD

Located at Central and Oliver streets in Wichita, Kansas, this mimetic structure was at one time quite the local attraction. During the decades before the onslaught of fast food, and the corporate chain stores, it was the one-of-a-kind eateries and snack stops that hooked the motorist to stop the car and spend. These days, it's ironic that the "educated" consumer abhors the unusual and embraces the nationally advertised, cookie-cutter products and brands. *Local History Section, Wichita Public Library*

WHITE CASTLE BUILDING

Doing business on the corner of Douglas and Hillside in Wichita, Kansas, this White Castle was the cat's meow when it came to shoveling down burgers (or sliders as they were often called) during the 1940s and 1950s. Unfortunately, none of the Wichita Castles has survived, the aromatic smells of boiling coffee and steaming beef patties exist only in the frames of documentary images. *Local History Section, Wichita Public Library*

of old appeared dated. With their rounded corners and their bulbous bodies, diners that the industry once heralded as "restaurants that looked fast" became only caricatures of speed. The rounded automobiles that once complemented their design were sitting idle in the junkyards.

As an unfortunate side effect of this aesthetic progress, many diner owners and manufacturers became convinced that their buildings could no longer look like they were diners. There were too many negatives to count on one hand: First and foremost, denigrators of the popular dining style regularly labeled them as "greasy spoons." Even the movies perpetuated the stereotype and depicted them as hangouts for the criminal element or an unsavory roost for ill-mannered truckers and other road scum.

In the quest to remain profitable and appeal to a wider, "family-style" audience, some suggested that the diner change its appearance to suit the times. To remain a viable business, it had to "fit in" with the rest of America's roadside architecture. As tastes changed, many decided that it was no longer good enough for an honest-to-goodness diner to be a practical, working eatery.

Oblivious to the magical treasures they possessed, many diner operators instituted a solemn campaign to disguise their eateries. One of the most common—and expedient—methods used to cover up a diner's personality was to encase it in an external cocoon. But this wasn't an architectural asset. The sad fact of the matter was that this process wasn't performed by skilled remodelers like the Erfred Corporation, but rather by mere weekend workers eager to make a buck.

With the hasty application of brick, siding, lath, and plaster, workers could transform a once-ostentatious O'Mahony or pompous Paramount into a benign building. As difficult as it is to believe from today's vantage point, many owners thought that this sort of conversion was the right thing to do for their business. Today, *Roadside* magazine denounces diners that owners and operators ruined by thoughtless "upgrading" by handing out

SPENCER'S SNACK SHOP

Spencer's Snack Shop was one of many Los Angeles eateries that endeavored to cater to the late 1940s motorist. Inspired by the long, lengthwise style of the typical diner building, Spencer's Snack Shop took a bold position on the outer envelope of roadside diner architecture with its unusual, albeit distinctive "hot dog in a bun" look. *Shades of LA/Los Angeles Public Library*

lunch cars, as did the refinishing or replacement of the outside skin.

Sometimes, the renovators removed all hints of the Streamline Moderne from those diners made during the 1930s and 1940s. As a replacement, they added a new, more angular exoskeleton to the body box. The Fedkenheuers achieved this new look by attaching alternating strips of stainless steel and Mirawal (a porcelain enameled product used by many of the new diner makers that came in 32 colors) to the outside. The new, up-to-date structure that emerged is today recognized by the diner experts as the signature work of the Erfred Corporation.

As diner owners scrambled to revamp their image, consumers looked toward the future and filled their minds with images of the space race. Automobile designers took their cue from the jet aircraft of the day and transferred the new aerodynamics to the car body. Now, when compared to the supersonic motif of the jet tailfin, the streamlining their "Lou-Roc Award," an honor given after a much-criticized makeover.

Acceptable or not, diner manufacturers caved in to the critics during the 1960s and began offering buildings that spoke the slang of new modernism. At the time, the designers at DeRaffele debuted their own futuristic diner, a unit of tight geometric lines that featured oversized panes of glass running from the lower third of the wall to the ceiling. With upward-flared plates and recessed lighting, the entrance migrated to the corner of the building. The industry took the cue and hard lines and sharp angles soon began to redefine the look of new diners.

Eager to blast into the future, other diner makers carried this look of hyped-up modern to the extreme. The zigzag roof style called the "folded plate" became a big hit with the builders of California coffee shops. (On the West Coast, diner operators took the path of the exaggerated modern, or "Googies" style of architecture.) Since it used up a lot of metal, steel makers could sell more material and diners eventually had to charge more for meals.

NICK'S GOOD FOOD DINER
Twenty years ago, residents of Front Royal, Virginia, frequented Nick's Good Food Diner when they wanted an economical meal. When it came to diners, Nick's was definitely one of a kind. What it lacked in style and flashy architecture it made up for with hand-lettered signs. Today, surviving examples of this sort of homespun advertising are few and far between.
Ronald Saari ©1999

Other diner makers toyed with the parabolic theme of the boomerang and many interior elements such as lamps and other fixtures took on a distinctive, flying saucer look. Signs and neon followed the form in an attempt to distract motorists from competing restaurant upstarts gathering momentum along the roadways. To everyone's amazement, the diner began to look less like an eatery and more like a spaceport. The Jetsons would be quite at home with a blue-plate special.

Ironically, this was not the most unattractive iteration of American diner architecture. During the 1970s, many diners continued the slow drive down the dead-end design street when they emerged from their chrysalis as lifeless, suburbanized buildings.

By the time John Travolta took the disco craze to its zenith in the movie *Saturday Night Fever*, the American diner dropped to the lowest depths of its design depravity. This signaled the unofficial end of the classic diner motif and the beginning of what diner historians refer to as the Colonial movement.

Suddenly, diners were no longer contiguous in their interior and exterior appearance. There were Colonial constructs, Pseudo-Grecian monuments, space-age temples, and a rogue's gallery of other styles that clouded the consumer's mind. The mansard roof became a standard, and practically all new commercial buildings, eateries and retail, attempted to blend into the blandness of a new roadside. Diners were losing their identity and, along with it, their soul. It was appropriate not to use the word "diner" anymore when one referred to them.

Now, owning a restaurant that looked like an old-fashioned diner was a liability. For some, it meant that your eatery was second class, a blue-collar has-been without any future. As a result, a large number of the unique, classy, one-of-a-kind, quaint, decorous diners of the golden years took on an appearance just like thousands of other restaurants that clogged the nation's highways.

Lauded by the industry critics and denounced by the diner die-hards, the streetside lunch car had reached the supposed pinnacle of its architectural expression. Fast food was now taking all the accolades and the diner was losing out—hanging on for dear life. Sitting in smoky booths and perched on counters, the fans of real diners were looking down the road in disgust, asking the same question: Is the American diner dying out?

THE SUPREME DINER

The Supreme Diner in West Springfield, Massachusetts, was a geometric stainless steel unit built by the DeRaffele Diner Manufacturing Company. For the last 10 years it was a Chinese restaurant, with the stainless painted a garish yellow and red. In 1998, it was bought and then moved to Cleveland, Ohio, by diner guru Steve Harwin. Currently, it's in storage or in the process of being restored to its former glory. *Pedar Ness ©1999*

Peter Pan Diner
U. S. ROUTE 40 & 13 — New Castle County Air-Port
New Castle, Delaware

PETER PAN
DINER
AIR CONDITIONED

Milk Shakes
and Pastries
Sundaes
& Sodas

Home
of the "B-29" BURGER

PETER PAN

PETER PAN DINER

New Castle, Delaware (right along U.S. Route 40 and Route 13), was the home of the Peter Pan Diner and the "B-29 Burger." During the 1950s, long before the age of elaborate theme parks, American roadside businesses held the job of entertaining the masses. *Courtesy Brian Butko*

THE BUCKHEAD DINER

Atlanta, Georgia, is the home of the Buckhead Diner, a homemade diner marvel built in 1987 that pushes the outer envelope of architectural design. An inverted stack of stepped parapets—finished out in ribbed bands of polished stainless steel and linear strips of neon tubing—gives this building the look of another world. *Andre Jenny ©1999/Unicorn Stock Photos*

Instilled with a sense of history and style that ordinary fast-food eateries find difficult to incorporate, today's diners (old, new, and restored) are back with a force that not even the experts could have predicted. Even the venerable McDonald's hamburger chain is experimenting with the diner concept. In 1998, McDonald's opened what it called a "Golden Arch Cafe" (really an imitation stainless steel diner) in Hartsville, Tennessee, about 40 miles outside of Nashville.

As Ronald McDonald is surely aware, today's bubbling interest in diners didn't boil up overnight. The reawakening began during the final years of the disco decade when authors, artists, and filmmakers took the diner to heart and began incorporating it into their work. In 1979, diner historian (and one-time diner restorer) Richard Gutman and photographer Elliott Kaufman set the kindling on fire when they published their seminal book *American Diner*.

In the years leading up to this book, photorealism artist John Baeder—described as a "poet-painter who makes us see the beauty of common things"—gained notoriety with his amazing diner paintings. When publisher Harry N. Abrahms

DINER STOOLS REDUX
Everything that's inside a diner isn't necessarily plated with chrome or made of burnished stainless steel. Sometimes, the right combination of painted metal and porcelain tiling creates a warm atmosphere that draws you in. Such is the case at the Adams Antique Market Diner in Adamstown, Pennsylvania. *Keith Baum ©1999*

PARK WEST DINER
Opening eyes in West Paterson, New Jersey, this new Kullman diner can be described as nothing less than an architectural tour de force. Look out: Kullman is back with a vengeance and taking no prisoners. Today, the American diner is all grown up and willing to rise to the challenge of beating out the fast food competition. Let the grill wars begin! *Jeff Greenberg/Unicorn Stock Photos*

debuted his book called *Diners*, the public's awareness grew even more.

When the Barry Levinson coming-of-age film *Diner* opened in the movie theaters in 1982, the smoldering interest in the mom-and-pop restaurants that took full advantage of neon tubing, long serving counters, cozy booths, padded stools, terrazzo floors, and a prodigious amount of stainless steel began to burn like a grease fire. Diners were on their way back, rising in popularity.

Against some heavy odds, all the books, movies, and magazine articles captured the essence of the diner as a restaurant form and repackaged it into a palatable entree for the masses. The upshot: Diners became a tasty social phenomenon and businesses that had undeniable appeal in modern culture.

Suddenly, a new audience of consumers wanted to visit eateries like the ones they saw in the movies. People wanted to find the old places like the Fells Point Diner again and hang out—just like actors Mickey Rourke, Kevin Bacon, Steve Guttenberg, Daniel Stern, Timothy Daly, and Ellen Barkin did on the silver screen.

And why shouldn't they? That unique sense of place, camaraderie, and community were qualities unattainable at the drive-through service lanes of the neighborhood McDonald's stand. The sit-down, take-your-time, elbows-on-the-counter, have-a-piece-of-apple-pie-honey,let-me-pour-you-another-cup-of-coffee diner represented the very best of American car culture cuisine.

By the mid-1980s, a definite resurgence in diners swept the nation. Restaurant operators who didn't cling to preconceived notions about the restaurant business acted on their urge to open new diners. At the same time, owners polished up those vintage gems that weathered the merciless onslaught of franchise food stands with newfound pride. Suddenly, diners were in vogue again. Best of all, some of the nostalgic diner scenes that found their way onto celluloid and canvas made

the jump from the realm of imagination into reality. Eating out in America had come full circle, and now it was the diner's turn to get the attention.

As always seems to happen when a new trend is "discovered," the big money muscled its way in and proceeded to create what the pundits called the "upscale" version—the "upscale diner." In 1984, Richard Melman of Lettuce Entertain You Enterprises was one of the first to realize the profit potential in the diner mystique when he debuted a diner-like eatery based on a mythical diner character named Ed Debevic (a neon caricature of the made-up greasy spoon owner was used in the Ed Debevic's sign). Californians loved it and soon others were opened in big cities such as Chicago.

That year, Philip Adelman moved a classic 1954 Mountain View diner from the town of Massillon to Cincinnati, Ohio, and tried his luck in the food business, adding on an expansive dining room that was big enough to seat 140 customers. One year later, a group doing business as Real Restaurants opened the gleaming doors of the Fog City Diner in the City By the Bay, San Francisco. To the delight of local gourmands, the outfit introduced nouvelle California cuisine to diners. Compared to the simple comfort food diners of yesteryear, this wasn't the same old meatloaf. Diners were learning new culinary tricks with the public as beneficiary.

The resurgence continued and recently, a deluge of diner wannabes have joined in the fray and

THE 66 DINER

With its Streamline Moderne style and colorful neon, the Route 66 Diner has become a new classic along the Mother Road. This Albuquerque, New Mexico, restaurant was recently damaged by fire, but plans are in the works to rebuild. *Howard Ande ©1999*

PHIL'S OLD DINER

Constructed by Charles Amend, a former employee of the Tierney Company who moved west, Phil's diner is the oldest diner in the California region. Recently, Charles and Wende Hong (they owned the eatery for 20 years) sold out because of waning business. The new owners have plans in the works to restore the classic and reopen it for the North Hollywood customers. *Kent Bash ©1999*

CROSSER DINER

Located in Lisbon, Ohio, the Crosser Diner is just about the most interesting, porcelain panel-clad, rectangular diner one could ever come across. High above on the brick wall, visitors may still see the fading "Crosser's Service Station and Diner" sign painted so many years ago. *Ronald Saari ©1999*

proffered restaurant plans for all those dizzy with "diner fever." At the end of the 1990s, Diner Concepts is building a really cool line of reproduction restaurant units under its catchy-sounding Diner-Mite brand. Directed by President David Bernstein, designers at this Atlanta, Georgia, company have devised a flexible line-up of modern diners that are capable of seating from 37 to 260 people.

Using steel construction throughout and advanced modular technology, the Diner-Mite diners are sturdy and easily moved to their intended business sites. The new "Blue-Plate Special" sports a 40-seat capacity inside a tiny footprint of 60x16 feet. It's the perfect choice for the modern diner man: pots, pans, grill, dishwasher, and kitchen equipment—everything except the waitress—

come as a turn-key package for $169,500.

A similar diner enterprise has gained converts in the franchise world too. Based in Mesa, Arizona, The 5 & Diner Franchise Corporation is marketing its reproduction diner packages to prospective restaurateurs who want to get in on a proven plan for serving food, without having to reinvent the meat slicer. For a franchise fee of $25,000 and a royalty payment of 5 percent thereafter, interested diner guys and diner gals can jump in on the ground floor of a growing chain. (Diner construction costs and necessary working capital boost the investment above $250,000.) To date, there are three 5 & Diners serving up their own style of western hospitality in Arizona, and a fourth operating in the tourist town of Reno, Nevada.

Meanwhile, back on the East Coast—that bastion of American dinerdom—industry stalwarts have rediscovered the age-old idea of good service and good taste. Out of the original list of diner manufacturers who used to market their wares from factories located there, three have withstood the tidal wave of fast food and today continue to turn out desirable products.

The well-respected DeRaffele Manufacturing Company of New Rochelle, New York, remains a competitor, as does a company diner buffs know as Paramount Modular Concepts of Oakland, New Jersey. (Remember the heavily stylized and eye-grabbing wedding-cake motifs of the 1950s? DeRaffele dreamed them up.)

Further along the New Jersey Turnpike in the town of Avenel, Kullman Industries remains a vibrant voice amid the cacophony of emerging diner makers. Founded in 1927 when accountant Sam Kullman quit P. J. Tierney and Sons to start his own diner company, Kullman boasts a record unmatched in the restaurant industry. When business dropped off during the 1960s, Kullman remained profitable by concentrating its efforts on the construction of other portable buildings.

SILVER DINER COUNTER

The interior of the new Silver Diners have all of the feeling of the classic 1950s diners and then some. The major difference here is the feeling—the overall intensity of the atmosphere. Go ahead, Mac, turn up the neon lights and crank up some tunes on the jukebox. I think that's Elvis sitting in the end booth. *Doug Brown ©1999/Courtesy of Silver Diner Development Inc.*

CRUISER'S DRIVE-IN

Cruiser's Drive-In is an unusual middle America hybrid: It combines the basic layout of the typical diner and marries it with the drive-in format. What's more, it adds a dash of the 1950s walk-up hamburger stand and believe it or not, a grain silo (made of glass block and topped with galvanized metal). Wagons Ho! It's time to eat in Crest Hill, Illinois. *Howard Ande ©1999*

Today, Kullman is back—bending new sheet metal and laying glass block, using the same tried-and-true methods it perfected during the diner heyday to manufacture an entirely new line of diners. The burgeoning craze for diners revived the specialty in 1987, the same year Kullman constructed the American City Diner on Connecticut Avenue in Washington, D.C. This was the first stainless steel diner the company had built in years, a model that brought the company back to the classic designs of the 1950s and revived the styling cues of the 1930s and 1940s.

Today, the jewel in its crown is a fantastic flashback dubbed the "Blue Comet," a sparkling eatery named after the famous passenger train that ran from Jersey City to Atlantic City during the 12 years between 1929 and 1941. It's a bona-fide dream of a diner, initially created with the assistance

of diner historian Richard Gutman and restaurant designer Charles Morris Mount.

The concept behind the new design was simple: Use skilled craftsmen to produce a transportable, beautiful, "Jersey-style" diner that appealed to the established markets in the Northeast and other areas of the country. Like some of its larger cousins that are still operating along the highways and byways of the Garden State, the Blue Comet had to hold its own when it came to layout, looks, and everyday restaurant functionality.

In all these areas, it succeeded. The cobalt blue-and-stainless steel beauty captures the real heart of the old diner-days diner and tempers it with all the updated needs of the modern restaurateur and businessman. Customization is the key and buying one has much in common with buying a luxury automobile. Customers can choose from all sorts of options, including an array of color patterns, type of kitchen design, accessories, and the number of seats (the base-model Comet seats 90).

In parallel to the car-buying experience, the prospective diner man or woman need not ask how much: The package price of one of these beauties can spiral well up into the hundreds of thousands of dollars—depending on options, floor plan, and configuration.

Even so, it makes sense to pay for quality, and Kullman has no shortage of interested buyers. The year 1997 proved to be the biggest growth period in the company's history, and the company's future looks as bright as polished stainless. According to Kullman sales representative Christopher Carvell, "The Blue Comet is a great lead-in for those interested in diners. First introduced to our company through the promotion of the Blue Comet, what

we've ended up with is a client who comes away with a structure more customized in terms of fitting their needs. The final product turns out to be a lot more elaborate than the Blue Comet." To date, Kullman has constructed a number of variations, ensuring that the diner mystique will live on for decades to come.

New Kullmans have joined their vintage brethren along the roadside, and prospective diner operators are taking a closer look. Robert Giaimo, the co-founder of Rockville, Maryland's Silver Diners, began his own operation with a Kullman. His flagship Silver Diner unit was built by the company (this was the second new diner built by the New Jersey

THE WILDWOOD DINER

It's more than possible that Bruce Springsteen ate a meal or two at the Wildwood Diner (Wildwood, New Jersey). This is the most southern end of Jersey and a favorite destination for hungry visitors to the shore, rockers included. *Ronald Saari ©1999*

diner maker in 1987). Inspired, he moved to other designs but retained the essence of the original, combining the look of the past with modern features of today, creating a line of diners that cast an imposing shadow along the Miracle Mile.

Giaimo is a perfect example of a modern diner success story with a corporate twist: He started a small restaurant chain called the American Cafe during the 1970s and sold 70 percent of his stake in 1989 to enter the diner business. He studied the

format at great length and along with partner and chef Ype Hengst, opened his first diner in Rockville. Excluding the cost of land, the enterprise cost the team around $2 million.

The investment was worthwhile: During the first year of business, Giaimo and his partner served 12,000 customers a week. Gross receipts totaled nearly $4 million. Since then, Giaimo added one Silver Diner a year, building six Silver Diner restaurants in suburban areas of Maryland and Virginia. "The rebirth of the diner is being fueled by a growing nostalgia for what is familiar and comfortable and by a dissatisfaction with the anonymous eating experiences of fast-food restaurants," he says.

In 1994, Giaimo realized what he calls "every entrepreneur's dream" when his diner concept hit

BENDIX DINER

The Bendix Diner is well known by those in Hasbrouck Heights, New Jersey, and by diner buffs across America. It's a Master diner built in 1947, one that's been featured in more than its share of television commercials, including spots for Reebok, Kellogg's Bran Flakes, U.S. Healthcare, Tonka, Coca-Cola, Maalox, and more. A few movie scenes were even shot there, including *Boys on the Side* and *Jersey Girl. Ronald Saari ©1999*

the corporate big time. One night, an investor dropped in unannounced and handed over a $14.2 million check for a stake in the company! This was investor and entrepreneurial idea man George Naddaff, the man who developed the successful Boston Chicken chain from a single store.

As the story goes, he "discovered" the Silver Diner chain in December of that year when he motored past the Rockville Pike location. "There was something absolutely stunning about this particular diner," Naddaff recalls. He stopped the car, got out, waited in line with the crowds waiting to get in, had a meal, looked over the kitchen, and even pilfered one of the oversized menus. The Silver Diner met his standards. With four restaurants operating at the time, it looked like it was a proven concept.

One year later, the last of several complex approvals was completed as shareholders of Boston-based Food Trends Acquisition Corporation (renamed Silver Diner Development Inc.) approved the purchase of the operation, giving Silver Diner shareholders 57 percent ownership in the new company. The Rockville-based chain became a public entity, with shares trading on the Nasdaq stock exchange. With that milestone accomplished, more plans are in the works: The Silver Diner was expected to expand to other East Coast markets in 1998 (as this book went to press), including Philadelphia and Florida. Later, the company will consider diner franchises.

Despite all of the architectural grandeur, the extensive menus punctuated by heart-healthy foods,

and vintage styling of these modern diner marvels, there are many enthusiasts who choose to avoid the diner neophyte. They simply favor the older, more-vintage eateries over the new ones. For them, it's a worthwhile endeavor to only take breakfast, lunch, or dinner in an original, "old tyme" diner, the kind of joint run by the same family since the year wheels were first removed from the lunch wagons.

Fortunately, there are a few dedicated diner men who are coming forward to restore yesterday's broken-down diners and keep them cooking. Hailing from Alpena, Michigan, restorer Al Sloan is one of them. Recently, he has gained recognition for his excellent efforts in the field of diner preservation. In 1994, his knack for bringing back diners from the dead reached a crest when he acquired Sandy's

Diner (also known as Sidetrack Cafe and Town Talk) of Hudson, Massachusetts. He discovered the tiny, porcelain panel, nine-stool Worcester Lunch Car Company model (circa 1925) disguised as part of another building and cloaked in vinyl siding. He purchased the time-machine and had mover O. B. Hill truck it to Alpena, where he began the major effort to revive it.

He didn't stop there: His current master-piece is a mirror-finish 1955 O'Mahony, a work-ing diner that enjoyed a working life in Wilkes-Barre, Pennsylvania. Previous owners called it Susanne's Diner, and locals previously knew it as the Chow Tyme Diner. He bought this metal-clad, Streamline Moderne marvel for the price of a
continued on page 142

LAMY'S DINER

Diner aficionados may travel to Dearborn, Michigan, to get a taste of what diners used to be like in the early days. At the Henry Ford Museum and Greenfield Village, visitors can take a gander at Lamy's Diner. It's part of the exhibit called "The Automobile in American Life." Shown here is the interior of the beautifully restored, 1946-vintage Worcester Lunch Car. *Ronald Saari ©1999*

RIVERHEAD GRILL

THE RIVERHEAD GRILL
85 East Main Street ★ Riverhead, New York

During the 1930s, the town of Riverhead, Long Island, boasted a busy and bustling Main Street. It was the typical scene of American prosperity: a variety of shops lined the way, including a Sears Roebuck, a food market, beautician, barber shop, and drugstore. In town, the local soda fountain and ice cream shop was a major draw. Residents enjoyed cruising down the Main Street strip for refreshments, as did the countless vacationers, duck hunters, fishermen, and automotive travelers "just passing through."

In 1932, John Moustaka figured he could take advantage of this growing market, and he placed his first ad in The Riverhead News for his new eatery, the Riverhead Grill. As indicated by the ad copy, he planned a first-class operation: "Only the best food, prepared under the personal supervision of an experienced chef will be served at Riverhead Grill. Both counter and table service. Special tables reserved for ladies." Main Street was getting its first diner.

When the doors opened a few weeks later, a crowd of hungry customers showed their satisfaction. The Grill's reputation for flavorful food and good service grew so rapidly that within five years, Moustaka had to expand. In 1937, he

RIVERHEAD GRILL POSTCARD
In 1932, when the Riverhead Grill first opened its doors on 85 East Main Street in Riverhead, New York, restaurants were quite different from those of today. In cities, diners positioned perpendicular to the street often featured an overhanging roof to protect arriving patrons from the elements. Unfortunately, as real estate on either side was sold and buildings constructed, the diner lost its identity, and the view from inside. *Courtesy of Liz Strebel*

moved the original building aside to make room for a shiny, stainless steel structure (shipped from New Jersey). To accommodate customers, he converted the old building into a kitchen and linked it with the new diner.

For the next 30 years, Moustaka perfected his diner operation and made it a prime example of the best. By 1961, he was an old hand in the business and knew how to please hungry customers. He was ready to hang up his apron.

At that time, ownership was transferred to two brothers, Joseph and Frank Strebel. They knew what the American dream was all about as their father had immigrated from Switzerland, eager for a prosperous life in the states. The pair had some restaurant experience: Since 1946, Joseph operated a place called Joe's Lunch on New York's Second Avenue. He was ready to trade in city life for small town charm.

By the time the Strebels took over, the Main Street section of Riverhead had grown. Now, it included an A&P supermarket, multiple shoe stores, beauty shops, and a brand new McCrory's store (to replace the aging Sears Roebuck). Presiding over the opposite side of the street was Woolworth's, the grand dame of all five-and-dimes.

was once a gleaming, stainless steel dream.

Even so, the spirit of this Main Street landmark couldn't be silenced. While outside the disco generation gyrated to a new beat, inside time stood still. At the core of the Grill beat the heart of a genuine diner. The front counter still provided stools from which customers could eat their meals and watch the grillmeister work his craft. A smiling waitress still welcomed locals with a nod and a "good to see you, Sam!" There was still plenty of time to chat about the weather, hometown events, and changing times. The food was still the same, including the quality and taste.

It was during this transitional period that Joe and Frank Strebel decided to hang up their spatulas, and in 1973, they received an offer to buy the diner. Now a young woman, Elizabeth Strebel wouldn't have it. She wanted to buy the business and keep the legacy of the Riverhead Grill in the family. She rose to the challenge and managed to keep the place running, using the same ingredients that her father and uncle used in the early days to make it such a tremendous success: enthusiasm, good food, hospitality, and energy.

Nevertheless, she couldn't stop progress. While life continued inside the diner, death crept along Main. One by one, stores shut their doors. Rows of buildings became empty shells with their windows boarded over. In 1997, even Woolworth's gave in to economic pressure and closed. The once-proud five-and-dime became a ghost of the past.

Today, the merchants, traffic, and shoppers are all gone. Route 58 guides cars to malls and supermarkets. Devoid of fancy shops, renovated stores, or antique malls—Riverhead has little to offer the consumer, except for one thing: the Riverhead Grill. People who know good food are still drawn in to sup at Elizabeth's diner where a good honest meal is served with a smile. Is the American Main Street dead? Not in this neck of Long Island. Elizabeth Strebel and the Riverhead Grill are making sure of that.

Joseph Strebel's family grew and by this time included four daughters. As it happened, it was his 11-year-old daughter, Elizabeth, who was first drawn to the business. She spent all her free time in the diner, watching her dad and Uncle Frank work their shtick at the grill. Outside, the wonder of Main Street beckoned, but she ignored the call. For her, all of the best action took place right inside the lively diner.

By the time she reached her teens, Elizabeth was on the Riverhead staff and was later joined by her three sisters. By 1966 the Riverhead Grill became a bona fide family operation as dad, uncle, and the teenagers worked together to please the customers and make the meals fun and enjoyable.

Unfortunately, the good times didn't last. Inflation reared its ugly head during the early 1970s, and a simple meatloaf platter that previously cost 95 cents shot up to $1.35. The new decade brought with it more serious changes as well: No longer were humble diners the cherished icons of roadside culture. Many—including the Riverhead Grill—were seen as outdated, unwanted reminders of the past.

Glitzy chain and fast-food restaurants ruled the roadways. As diner owners scrambled to save their failing businesses, many succumbed to the temptation of revamping their exteriors. The theory was that if all traces of their origin were erased, business wouldn't suffer.

The Riverhead Grill followed the crowd. Workers covered its worn diner exterior with a layer of brick and siding. To further hide its lineage, renovators installed a bay window. The new shell provided an ample layer of camouflage and to this day, few can tell that the Riverhead Grill

MICKEY'S DINER

Mickey's Dining Car is located at Seventh and St. Peter streets in St. Paul, Minnesota. The diner is a 1937 O'Mahony, now listed on the National Register of Historic Places. This will ensure a secure future for the eatery, despite its city setting and the rising value of surrounding real estate. It's been open every day, 24 hours a day, since 1940. *Ronald Saari ©1999*

FREEHOLD GRILL

Freehold, New Jersey, is where the diner seeker has to travel to grab a steaming cup of coffee and slice of blueberry pie at the Freehold Grill. This 1950s O'Mahony is located right along Main Street. Be sure to come after dark and behold the magic of the amazing neon sign. *Ronald Saari ©1999*

continued from page 139
fine luxury vehicle and had it transported in two sections to new digs in Alpena. There, he carefully restored the structure inside and out and renamed it Al's. Smitten, Sloan decided to take a stab at the restaurant end of the diner business. Today, Al's is a working diner with one very enthusiastic owner.

Steve Harwin's story is similar: Once an ardent restorer of exotic cars, he got hooked on diners back in 1990 and never quite shook the addiction. With an obsessive attention to the smallest details and an endless patience for restoration work, he has single-handedly rescued a long list of diner treasures from the oblivion of the junk pile.

Today, he's the one to talk to if you are even thinking about buying and restoring a diner.

His work speaks for itself, and mere words don't do justice to his list of retro-redux. The best way to get a sense of his restoration art is to inspect them in person and sit down in one of the booths. Recent diner accomplishments in the renovation arena: reworking the Ono Diner into the Big Dig in Boston; saving the Zephyr Diner (reopened as the all-dessert Sweet City in Cleveland); providing diners for Ruthie and Moe's in Cleveland (same town); and saving the diminutive Short Stop diner (once located in Belleville, New Jersey, the hamburger bar is now stored at Harwin's diner yard in Cleveland). "This is

history," he declared in a *Spirit* magazine interview. "You can't throw away history."

Diner restoration expert Daniel Zilka deserves kudos as well. Not only does he make a living out of restoring diners, he spends his free time in pursuit of another worthy diner goal: preserving diner history. Zilka is currently the primary booster for The American Diner Museum (www.dinermuseum.org) of Providence, Rhode Island, an organization formed as "a tribute to the individuals who built, operated and worked in diners and to those who continue the diner tradition into the 21st century." Through his efforts, current diner fans can rest assured that the diner's past, present, and future history will pass on to the future generations.

The American Diner Museum is one of the most ambitious diner collections to date, with plans to offer patrons interactive video displays and exhibits commemorating numerous diner manufacturers. An on-site reference library will provide public access to vintage company literature, records, and historic photographs. Long-range plans call for diner tours, restoration workshops, a diner shop, and of course, a diner exhibit. An actual, full-scale classic diner will be the focal point of the exhibit.

PECK DRUG COMPANY

During the early 1940s, the Bastion Blessing Company manufactured a number of different art deco–inspired stool-and-counter unit backbar designs. This blue setup was the interior of Peck's Drug Company in Grand Rapids, Michigan. *Coolstock ©1999*

144

It's all part of the former South Street Power Station building that's located in the revitalized downtown riverfront district of Providence (the city where the diner began). Under the direction of the Providence Historical Society, the facilities for the "Heritage Harbor Museum and Library" are being refurbished now. Plans call for a grand opening early in the new millennium.

Until then, there are other promoters of the diner archetype spreading the gospel of counter-culture, particularly in print. Whether a diner is

new, old, refurbished, or retro, a niche publication called *Roadside* magazine covers them all. A labor of love dedicated to a simpler America, it's published in Worcester, Massachusetts, by Randolph Garbin's Coffee Cup Publications.

Most savvy diners on the East Coast (and in other regions) carry free issues of the magazine just so they can hand them out to the customers. Of course, most of the real diner enthusiasts are subscribers. It's easy to see why, as Garbin's trademarked recipe for an American renaissance is eloquent, yet simple: "Eat in diners; Put a porch on your house; Ride trains; Shop on Main Street; Live in a walkable community."

Roadside is the barometer of today's diner industry. Every quarter, it features a variety of stories on current diners (and their status) and it runs

ARLINGTON DINER

Located in North Arlington, New Jersey, the Arlington Diner was famous for its cheesecake. The building was a typical example of the modern style of Colonial architecture. Open 24 hours, it beckoned customers to enter beneath its unusual, upwardly angled roof line. *Preziosi Postcards*

145

MODERN LIDO DINER

In terms of modern design, the Lido didn't miss the boat: a diamond, rear-lit, tri-decorative assembly was mounted above the entrance and space-age angular support posts adorned the sides. In front were huge, expansive windows and large panels of stainless steel. Whereas the normal diner entrance was rather nondescript, the Lido's ostentatious, futuristic entryway had a lot more in common with an elaborate stage setting befitting a Buck Rogers serial. *Courtesy of Guy Kudlemyer*

a section called "Napkin Notes" that dishes up the latest happenings in dinerdom. Armed with a copy of the magazine (they even have a colorful presence on the worldwide web (www.roadsidemagazine.com), diner aficionados can keep up with their favorite haunts, see which ones remain open, track how they are changing, where they are moving, and what kind of food they are serving. At the same time, modern-day denizens of the diner can stoke up on a sample of diner lore, countertop gossip, and history.

For those already in the business and those who want to get in, *Roadside* breaks the sad news about abandoned diners and those that might be sold. Readers can browse through the pages to locate the ultimate diner of their dreams: In each issue, featured diner finder maps point the hungry motorist to all of the eateries that are currently open for busi-

ness. On occasion, display ads feature the forgotten classics that are up for sale, along with a panoply of related goods that no diner operator can do business without. (The magazine also sells a list of available diners, with its companion volume, *Primer for Owning an American Institution.*)

With those thoughts in mind, there are many who believe that the diner is only a concept, a prepackaged idea that they can put in a can, market, and ship overseas. And so, much to the chagrin of the domestic diner enthusiasts and purveyors of pop archeology, many of our most precious diners are being shipped to Europe.

It happens mostly out of apathy and an unwillingness to take care of our own legacy: For months and often years, perfectly sound diners sit vacant or abandoned with no buyers in sight, and suddenly a

foreign interest comes along with a top-dollar offer. Foreign restaurateurs are in a wild feeding frenzy for mid-20th century American culture, and the interest continues to grow.

In 1992, a significant number of diners moved permanently out of the United States. In a highly publicized case, Uncle Will's diner in Shrewsbury, Massachusetts, and another abandoned eatery in Palmer made a run for the border. Both landed far to the north in Montreal, Canada, and came under the care of Daniel Noiseux. He restored them in Quebec, consulting with author and former diner restorer Richard Gutman to draft the interior plans.

If one puts aside all the notions of diner nationalism, it's easy to compliment the effort. One of the vintage diners was reborn as "Le Galaxie" and today it's drawing good crowds up in Montreal. It has proved itself to be a gleaming ambassador for American style and culture, decked out in rear-lit glass block, neon bands, and acres of stainless steel panel.

To date, the most visible proponent of this international expansion has been the Fatboy chain. In 1993, American diner fans were literally losing their lunch as the English company founded by Trevor Gulliver set out to acquire 40 American diners. Despite the cries from dinerdom that "there weren't that many good diners available," the company held that it wasn't really a cultural raid and added insult to injury when it announced that "saving these diners has not been done very well in the U.S.A." The company found a few available diners and opened a

THE FABULOUS FIFTIES

In 1986, Jeff Tay purchased a Happy Steak restaurant on Fair Oaks Boulevard in Carmichael, California. With the help of Michael and Linda Dunlavey of the Dunlavey Studio, a new design emerged for the eatery. On the exterior of the building, a 22-foot facade was constructed. A 1959 Cadillac and 1958 Edsel were "crashed" through, resting halfway in and out. Several national and state design awards were won for the bold departure. In the early 1990s, the eatery changed owners and re-emerged as a Mels Diner. *Courtesy of the Dunlavey Studio*

THE COUNTRY DINER

The Country Diner operated on High Ridge Road in Stamford, Connecticut, circa 1950s. New England's "Newest and Most Modern" diner, it featured all of the architectural pizzazz that the postwar diner designers could imagine. Not only was stainless steel used, but an upwardly canted, folded entrance canopy gave the structure a distinct feeling of the future (very curious, considering the "homey" name). Decorative chevrons mounted at the roofline hid rooftop equipment and echoed the modernistic tone. This was the decade of automotive tailfins, and it seemed like even roadside restaurants were taking their design cues from the lines of the American automobile. *Preziosi Postcards*

KULLMAN DINING CAR MATCHBOOK

Kullman has come a long way in the diner manufacturing industry and managed to come out on top. Once regarded as the "Builders of Better Type Dining Cars and Castle Turret Dinettes," Kullman Industries is striding into the 21st century with a line of diners that combines the practicality of the 1950s with the showmanship of a new millennium. *Preziosi Postcards*

trio of American-style diners in London. There are plans to open more.

In this same vein, the diner is making converts of those who used to oppose the ideals of capitalism. In 1996, *The Dallas Morning News* nipped the taste buds of Texas diner fans with the feature article "Meatloaf with a Russian Twist: Muscovites line up for down-home cooking at the Starlite Diner." American diner capitalism and communism meet— head on.

As reported by special contributor Betsy McKay, the city of Moscow has every kind of restaurant these days, from Mexican to French food. Now they even have a good-old American diner, open for service 24 hours a day. When Muscovites get the craving for gravy-drenched French fries or their favorite toasted Fluffernutter sandwiches, they can sit themselves down at the new Starlite Diner, located just minutes from the Kremlin.

Shawn McKenna, an American entrepreneur who owns another Moscow restaurant, had the diner (a reproduction with stainless steel exterior and all of the trimmings) transported to Russia from the Starlite facilities in Ormond Beach, Florida. "We're not bringing the new America to Russia; we're trying to bring what was right about the old America," he says. "It's a subtle, careful America, a time people want to remember."

At $7 a pop for an American-style cheeseburger and a golden-brown order of French fries, the Starlite is a welcome respite compared to Moscow's expensive, upscale eateries. There, restaurant dinners can often run as high as $100 per person.

Undeniably, the diner craze is a global phenomenon. Back in the states, all sorts of companies—from mail order to department store— are selling "cool stuff" that's based on the diner mystique. A recent *Car*

Culture catalog (the brainchild of car photographer Lucinda Lewis and Machine Age Inc.) featured the whimsical "Joe's Diner" phone, a fully functional gizmo packaged under the Telemania brand. Its removable diner roof serves as a handset. When lifted off the hook, the diner interior lights up. On incoming calls, the telephone plays Bill Hailey's "Rock Around the Clock" (instead of using a standard bell-style ringer).

The diner phone is an appropriate metaphor for diner-buying convenience, since one may now buy a diner simply by calling a toll-free number. Case in point: During the 1997 Christmas holiday season, the ritzy Neiman Marcus department store (based in Dallas, Texas) mailed out its yearly catalog, a glossy booklet that featured a fully equipped, operational diner!

As the catalog ad copy described the "gift," this flashback from the 1950s boasted "1950s styling and authentic details—from neon to memorabilia." Custom-built with stainless steel, it came with four booths, Formica-topped counter, and 11 bar stools (seating a total of 19 diners). The mail-order diner fantasy came complete with full food and beverage service and included the bar, microwave, ice machine, and an ice cream box with dipper. But there's more: The deal included a curved ceiling, interior ceramic tiling, remote-control Rock-Ola jukebox, a small dance floor, black-and-white checkerboard floor tiles, and last but not least, a central heating and air-conditioning system.

Interested holiday gift-givers hovering in the higher income brackets had to plunk down a deposit of $50,000 just to secure delivery. For the lucky few who could afford it, the diner was the perfect gift answer for that person on their list who had everything. The grand total of the entire nostalgia/food service package topped out at an impressive $195,000.

Really, the figures are relative. The amount of money that's now being spent on diner style is not a big surprise to nostalgia dealers. Consumers are so enamored with the diner "look" that they are fixing up their own dining rooms to appear as if they are real, working diner rooms—decked out with replica soda-serving counters, stools, reproduction jukebox radios, milkshake mixers, and booths covered in nothing less than genuine Naugahyde.

Immense electric clocks adorned with rings of neon are all the rage, as are vintage diner tableware, coffee mugs, napkin dispensers, vintage advertising thermometers, porcelain enameled signs, and even restored Coca-Cola machines. If you're a fan of Elvis, James Dean, Marlon Brando, Marilyn Monroe, and diners—all at the same time—there's an item just for you. It's a poster called the *Hollywood Diner*, a color lithograph take-off of Edward Hopper's famous "Nighthawks" painting that features all four of these film icons taking a stool at a mythical LA eatery.

Diners are popping up in other places, too, including the great expanse of cyberspace. Today, self-styled computer nerds have an ever-changing array of diner sites to pick from when browsing the Internet. When the urge strikes to visit a digital

THE AMERICANA DINER
Located in Shrewsbury, New Jersey, the Americana Diner is one of the new, large "New Jersey style" diners currently being built by Kullman Industries. In this model, the vestibule has reached dramatic proportions, a full 24 feet high. The exterior features an extensive use of glass block, a "horizontal pattern" of mirror-finish stainless steel (this popular motif used a satin finish during the 1950s), and a "double roll" roof (to hide mechanical systems such as air-conditioning). At 5,000 square feet, owner Jimmy Dimitroulakos is capable of seating about 150 happy patrons. *Courtesy Kullman Industries, Inc.*

JOHNNY D'S DINER

Johnny D's diner is one of the new Kullman breed. Owned by John Daskalis and doing business in New Windsor, New York, it features porcelain fluted panels and colorful Spandrel glass (used for its great reflective quality) as important design elements. While the outside captures the feeling of the 1940s and 1950s, the interior takes on the ambiance of a 1930s diner. Fine mahogany wood graces the walls and the ceiling. On the floor, a dramatic application of black, white, and gray marble tiling sets the nostalgic mood. *Courtesy Kullman Industries*

diner, the intrepid web surfer may browse the pages of working diner restaurants like Rosie's (www.rosiesdiner.com), Ruby's (www.rubys.com), Moody's (www.midcoast.com/~scottj/moody.htm), Jigger's (www.intap.net/~bozone/DNR/Jiggers.html), Zinn's (www.zinnsdiner.com), the Highland Park Diner (www.highlandparkdiner.com), Miss Bellows Falls Diner (www.say-i-do.com/diner/), and countless others.

For the more serious aficionados of road food, there are an endless number of diner off-ramps to visit along the information superhighway. Diner destinations like the author's Roadside Memories (http://home.earthlink.net/~mikwitz/index.html), Chrone's Virtual Diner (www.neb.com/noren/diner/Chrones.html), the Diner Waitress (www.suckmy-big.org/diner), Dave's Diner Homepage (www.astro. princeton.edu/~goldberg/diner.html), Diner City (www.dinercity.com), and Roadside (www.roadsidemagazine.com) offer a fun-filled cornucopia of news, photographs, and historical facts. Some are filled with useful material and great diner images, others blend in a plethora of arcane and off-

beat information. The sites change on daily, with new ones coming on line all the time. Many sites have long lists of diner-related links.

The counterculture appeal of roadside truck stops, diners, and greasy spoons doesn't end on the Internet. Even the everyday cast of characters who make up the diner scene are thrown into the spotlight, including the dishwasher, the lowliest of all

OLE GEHMAN'S DINER INTERIOR
Located in Ronks, Pennsylvania, Ole Gehman's Diner features the utilitarian interior details of the legendary Silk City diner line. There's a place for everything and everything is in its place. "Enjoy the Nostalgia of Diner Style Eating" was a recent ad slogan at Gehman's culinary flashback. *Michael Dregni ©1999*

METRO DINER GLASS BRICKS
In Tulsa, Oklahoma, the Metro Diner is just one of the new diner attractions that may be found along the "Mother Road," old Route 66. Locals and cross-country travelers who take the old highway stop in regularly to soak up the nostalgia and bask in the glow of neon tubing and reflective glass block. *Shellee Graham ©1999*

restaurant employees (even though the average diner really suffers without one on staff). During the 1990s, *Out West* newspaper broke the story on Dishwasher Pete, a guy with dishpan-hands aiming to trek the country and wash dishes in all 50 states.

Pete has washed and scoured his way across America, cleaning up plates in restaurants, hospitals, cafeterias, canneries, and other roadside eateries.

Averse to travel in his youth, he began his clean-up quest at the age of 18. One day, he just got the itch to leave home and drifted from state to state, enrolling in college from time to time (taking all kinds of courses) and washing dishes along the way—sometimes only long enough to cash one paycheck. Armed with a bottle of soap, a scrub brush, and a dish towel, Pete Jensen washed and scrubbed

the "loose meat" sandwich, Roseanne Barr and her television sister went into the diner business. On the show, they bought the Pizza Palace on Route 42 and reopened it as the Lanford Lunchbox.

In an ironic example of life imitating art, Barr and her then-real-life hubby, Tom Arnold, opened a similar eatery in Eldon, Iowa. They wanted to have a nice place to eat burgers and BLTs when they visited their nearby mansion and figured a diner was just the thing. Despite much attention from fans of the show, Roseanne and Tom's "Big Food" Diner later closed when the couple divorced.

In the same spirit of the memorable television show *Alice* (remember Mel the grumpy cook, the irascible Flo, and bumbling Vera?), other notable productions with diner settings or themes have aired on television as well. NBC unveiled a new program during

GIAIMO AT THE COUNTER

Robert Giaimo started a small restaurant chain called the American Cafe during the 1970s and sold most of his stake in 1989 to enter the diner business. He studied the format and along with partner (and chef) Ype Hengst, opened his first Silver Diner in Rockville, Maryland. During the first year of business, they served 12,000 customers a week. Since then, they have added one diner a year, building six Silver Diner restaurants in the suburban areas of Maryland and Virginia. *Courtesy of Silver Diner Development*

PHYLLIS' DINER, BOSTON

Small diners aren't extinct yet. Many diminutive operations survive to this day and still manage to sling hash in quiet neighborhoods across America. Phyllis' Diner is a good example: It operates outside of the city of Boston and continues to shrug off the specter of corporate domination. *Coolstock ©1999*

his way to 15 minutes of fame (but not monetary fortune, as pay for washing dishes ranges from $4.50 to $7.50 per hour, depending on locale). He even landed a guest shot with David Letterman.

Now, the airwaves have picked up on the widespread appeal of the diner. Every weeknight, a typical type of New York diner (with neon sign) hogs the screen during the opening minutes of the *Late Show with David Letterman*. Grinning from ear to ear, band leader Paul Shaffer and all the members of the CBS Orchestra enjoy themselves in the booths.

In another time slot, the fun continues: Comedian Jerry Seinfeld, along with screen characters Cosmo Kramer, Elaine Bennis, and George Costanza, frequent a local city-style diner as their choice to eat and to meet. (There's usually a lot more crazy talk going on in the booths than there is eating.) It's a popular hangout called Monk's Cafe, the celebrated Big Apple haunt of what was television's highest-rated comedy series, *Seinfeld*. In character, this diner is definitely a cultural hub. Eventually, anyone and everyone shows up there to discuss their problems.

A few years ago, the dream of owning a working-class diner earned notoriety as an attainable goal in the situation-comedy about a "domestic goddess," *Roseanne*. Based on an invention they dubbed

the 1997 fall prime-time line-up called *Union Square*, about a quirky New York diner that serves as the heart and soul of a downtown New York neighborhood.

In the diner, an eclectic mix of staff and regulars find a safe haven, a sounding board, and familiar faces. The cast of characters runs the gamut from an aspiring rock star to the world's worst waiter, with an up-and-coming screenwriter thrown into the blend. "Life is often lived in this sort of diner," says executive producer Marco Pennette. "It's a way station for people pursuing their dreams. Tom Cruise waited tables; David Mamet still writes plays at a booth in his local coffee shop."

Amplified by all the renewed interest generated by the visual media, original diner memorabilia and ephemera are now big collectibles. Linen and chrome postcards from the early diner days (all the way up to their low point during the 1970s) are hot commodities, as are vintage sales catalogs from defunct diner brands, photos, and copies of the hard-to-find industry magazine, *The Diner* (most were donated to the war effort during the 1940s).

Fortunately, there are more than enough other diner items to satisfy the rabid ranks of the present-day collector: swizzle sticks, matchbook covers, old menus, vintage equipment, diner furniture, and neon signs are fair game for the enthusiast.

What does it all mean? In the final analysis, when we take a long hard look at the hoarding of diner memorabilia, the valiant efforts for restoration, the extensive coverage in film, the obsession of artists, repeated air play on television, and the widespread use in advertising, it's obvious that the escalating interest in diners—and what they represent—points to a specific problem. All of these symptoms point to a greater ill.

It may be argued that the fascination with diners is a knee-jerk reaction to the demise of quality, the disappearance of great-tasting foods, and the extinction of casual eateries where the public may consume all of the above. "Dinermania" is not the abnormality of a few roadside eccentrics; it's a nationwide movement that hopes to recapture the ambiance of the diner.

To be frank, it's not really the diner that is in decline, it's the way of life begun by the diner men of yesterday. Taking lunch or dinner away from home is no longer an event, and more often than not, it's a real disappointment. Regional specialties are slowly dying. Using little imagination, restaurants duplicate the same meals, drinks, and desserts from coast to coast.

From the ever-changing taxpayer strips of California to the diner highways of New Jersey, American fast food has leveled off at what some critics believe is the lowest common denominator of choice. Along America's freeways, every exit ramp looks the same as another: Regardless of the state or region you are driving in, the modern-day traveler comes across the same signs, the same restaurants, and the same bill of fare.

These days, with all the corporate mergers and with family-owned restaurants going out of business, it's really not that unreasonable for the consumer to think that in 20 years, there might be only a single brand of eatery left, serving only one

5 & DINER OPERATIONS

Based in Mesa, Arizona, 5 & Diner is marketing its repro diner packages to prospective restaurateurs who want to get in on a proven plan for serving food, without having to reinvent the meat slicer. For a franchise fee of $25,000 and a royalty payment of 5 percent thereafter, interested diner guys and gals can jump in on the ground floor. *Courtesy of the 5 & Diner Franchise Corporation*

TABLETOP JUKEBOX CONTROLLER

The jukebox, or jukebox controller, has always been a familiar fixture at the diner (this model is a Seeburg Consolette at Mels Diner on Route 422 in Lebanon, Pennsylvania). By way of these handy machines, patrons could select a tune of their choice and hear it at the comfort of their own table or stool. In the days before the proliferation of personal headphones, having access to music while dining out was a novelty and luxury. *Larry Schulz 1999*

type of food. Think about the possibilities: Marketing experts might reduce the abbreviated menu found at your neighborhood fast-food hut to a few basic food items. New processing machines might extrude these meals from the same mixture of "food substance," irradiated and prepackaged "for the customer's convenience."

The horrific prediction for this kind of bland, uninspired future may be an exaggeration, but it's exactly this sort of direction that the diner is here to protect us from. After all, isn't a small measure of ambiance, taste, style, and authentic atmosphere what the American dining experience is about?

Isn't it more fun to break bread with friends and people you have come to know than anonymously gulping down a milkshake and burger in the front seat of your car? Why just settle for a greasy burger patty and lifeless bun when you can fill your tummy with a Cheeseburger Deluxe Platter? How

can a sandwich made with a faux rack of ribs compare to a full blue-plate special, a pot roast dinner delivered to your table by a real live waitress and not handed through a window? This is the kind of dining experience that anyone may enjoy at their favorite American Diner.

So come on, get in your automobile, break out the diner-finder map, and drive down to your local diner. Take a booth or a stool at the counter, become a regular, and absorb the atmosphere. Get to know your waitress. Make a point to memorize the lengthy menu, the songs on the jukebox, and the faces of employees. Witness for yourself the satisfied smiles of your fellow customers. Most important, be confident in your choice of eatery, as this is without a doubt the place to be when you want a heaping helping of good food, good friends, and fair prices. This, my fellow fans of roadfood, is the legacy of *The American Diner.*

WEST END DINER INTERIOR

The West End Diner is located in West Des Moines, Iowa. A modern restaurant with all the latest accouterments, it's satisfying the appetite (both with their food and with architecture) that middle America is developing for the diner. *Shellee Graham ©1999*

BIBLIOGRAPHY

"A Blast From the Past—Cafe an Explosion of Things '50s." *Identity* (Winter 1990): 28-31, 78.

Allen, Jane E. "White Tower Eatery Becomes Museum Piece." *Sunday News Journal*, Wilmington, Delaware (January 3, 1988): B7.

Anderson, Warren H. "Vanishing Roadside America." Tucson: The University of Arizona Press, 1981.

Anderson, Will. *Mid-Atlantic Roadside Delights*. Portland, Maine: Anderson and Sons Publishing Company, 1991.

New England Roadside Delights. Portland, Maine: Anderson and Sons Publishing Company, 1989.

Baeder, John. *Gas, Food, and Lodging: A Postcard Odyssey Through the Great American Roadside*. New York: Abbeville Press, 1982.

Diners. New York: Harry N. Abrahms, Inc., 1995.

Diners of New Jersey. Wayne, New Jersey: William Paterson College, 1978.

Bailey, Joanne. "Local Couple Transports Historic Diner to Grand Rapids Area." *ADA/Forest Hills Advance* (February 17, 1993).

"Back to the Future, Kentwood Couple Trucks '50s Diner Across Country to New Home." *ADA/Forest Hills Advance* (February 16, 1993): 1.

Baraban, Regina. "The Amazing Evolution of Fast Food." *Restaurant Design* (Winter 1981): 30-37.

Beebe, Lucius. *Mr. Pullman's Elegant Palace Car*. Garden City, New York: Doubleday and Company, Inc., 1961.

Belasco, Warren James. *Appetite for Change: How Counterculture Took on the Food Industry, 1966–988*. New York: Pantheon Books, 1989.

Blossfield, Tom. "Diner Moves In, Aims top 'Bring Back Tradition of '50s." *The Grand Rapids Press* (March 23, 1995): Business, A15.

Boas, Max, and Steve Chain. *Big Mac: The Unauthorized Story of McDonald's*. New York: E. P. Dutton and Company, Inc., 1976.

Brady, Tim. "Diner on the Corner, As Time Goes by, Mickey's Stands Still." *Minneapolis St. Paul* (May 1989): 80–81.

Browel, J. E. "How Safe is the Roadside Restaurant?" *Hygeia* 17 (July 1939): 590-2.

Campbell, Dana Adkins. "Yesterday's Sodas and Shakes." *Southern Living* 27 (February 1992): 130.

Childs, Leslie. "Hot Dog Kennels as Nuisances to Adjoining Property Owners." *American City* 63 (February 1928): 137.

Clarke, Blake. "Who is Howard Johnson?" *Reader's Digest* 55 (July 1949): 127–130.

Claudy, C. H. "Organizing the Wayside Tea House." *Country Life in America* 29 (June 1916): 54.

Clifford, J. C. "The Investor Views the Chain Restaurant." *The Magazine of Wall Street* (October 17, 1931): 848–872.

Cody, Larch. "Are Drive-Ins Being Driven Out?" *Los Angeles Herald-Examiner* (March 4, 1973) California Living: 9–10.

"Coffee and in the Doggy-Wagon." *Literary Digest* 112 (February 20, 1932): 43.

Coleman, Chrisena A. "So Long Pal's, Mahwah's 1950s Diner Being Shipped to Michigan." *North Jersey Record* (February 4, 1993): 2B.

"Coming . . . A New Restaurant Trend." *American Restaurant* 31 (April 1949): 125–126.

"The Complete Story of the Dining Car." Sales Brochure, Kullman Dining Car Company, Inc. (circa 1950s).

Daniels, Wade. "'Googie's Diner to Survive as Mels Opens on Sunset." *Los Angeles Business Journal* (September 22–28, 1997).

Dauphinais, Dean, and Peter M. Gareffa. *Car Crazy: The Official Motor City High-Octane, Turbocharged, Chrome-Plated, Back Road Book of Car Culture*. Detroit, Michigan: Visible Ink Press, 1996.

Diner. A Jerry Weintraub Production. Culver City, California: MGM/UA Home Video, 1982.

The Diner. June 1940 to November 1941, July 1946 to June 1950. Plainfield, New Jersey: Laurel Publications.

The Diner and Counter Restaurant. July 1950 to December 1951. Plainfield, New Jersey: Laurel Publications.

Diner and Restaurant. January 1952 to December 1953. Plainfield, New Jersey: Laurel Publications.

Diner-Drive-In and Restaurant. January 1954 to April 1955. Plainfield, New Jersey: Laurel Publications.

Diner-Drive-In. May 1965 to December 1959. Plainfield, New Jersey: Laurel Publications.

Divine, Charles. "The Thousand and One Night Owls." *The New York Times Magazine* (December 24, 1922): 8.

Dubin, Murray. *South Philadelphia: Mummers, Memories, and the Melrose Diner*. Philadelphia, Pennsylvania: Temple University Press, 1996.

Ehle, Henry S. "Do New Super-Roads Doom Restaurants?" *American Restaurant* 42 (June 1959): 51–58.

Eiss, Albert. "Carhop Service—Yes Or No?" *Restaurant Management* (June 1960): 32, 130, 132.

"Elevating the Standing of the 'Hot Dog Kennel'" *American City* 38 (May 1928): 99–100.

Emerson, Robert L. "Fast Food: The Endless Shakeout." New York: Lebhar-Friedman Inc., 1979.

Erlich, Blake. "The Diner Puts on Airs." *Saturday Evening Post* 220 (June 19, 1948): 34–35.

Farb, Peter, and George Armelagos. *Consuming Passions: The Anthropology of Eating*. New York: Houghton Mifflin Company, 1980.

Farhi, Paul. "Mels Diner Making S.F. Comeback." *San Francisco Examiner* (August 27, 1987): Business section.

Fengler, May. *Restaurant Architecture and Design*. New York: Universe Books, 1969.

Finch, Christopher. *Highways to Heaven: The Auto Biography of America*. New York: HarperCollins Publishers Inc., 1992.

Flink, James J. *The Automobile Age*. Cambridge, Massachusetts: The MIT Press, 1988.

The Car Culture. Cambridge, Massachusetts: The MIT Press, 1975.

Frazer, Elizabeth. "The Destruction of Rural America: Game, Fish and Flower Hogs." *The Saturday Evening Post* (May 9, 1929): 39, 193-194, 197–198.

Furniss, Ruth MacFarland. "The Ways of the Tea House." *Tea Room Management* 1 (August 1922): 5.

Garbin, Randolph; editor. *Roadside* magazine, various issues from 1989 to present. Watertown, Massachusetts: Coffee Cup Publications, 1998.

Garfunkel, Louis X. *Sandwich Shops, Drive-Ins and Diners: How to Start and Operate Them*. New York: Greenberg Publisher, 1955.

Gaseau, Michelle. "Diner to Go, Hold the Mustard." *The Marlborough and Hudson Enterprise Sun* 104:213 (May 21, 1994): 1, 8.

Gebhard, David, and Harriette Von Breton. *L.A. in the Thirties*. New York: Peregrine Smith Inc., 1975.

Genovese, Peter. *Jersey Diners*. New Brunswick, New Jersey: Rutgers University Press, 1996.

Genthner, Nancy Moody. *What's Cooking at Moody's Diner: 60 Years of Recipes and Reminiscences*. West Rockport, Maine: Dancing Bear Books, 1989.

Gibbons, Gail. *Marge's Diner.* New York: T. Y. Crowell, 1989.

Green, Blake. "Mel on Wheels: The '50s Return." *San Francisco Chronicle* (September 15, 1986): 40–42.

Gunnel, John A., and Mary L. Sieber. *The Fabulous Fifties: The Cars, The Culture.* Iola, Wisconsin: Krause Publications, 1992.

Gutman, Richard J.S., and Elliot Kauffman, in collaboration with David Slovic. *American Diner.* New York: Harper and Row, 1979.

Gutman, Richard J.S. *American Diner, Then and Now.* New York: HarperCollins Publishers Inc., 1993.

Haber, Alan. "DINER Serves Up Promotional Dollars." *Radio World* (January 11, 1995)" 26–36.

Heavy. Presented by Available Light. Culver City, California: Columbia TriStar Home Video, 1997.

Heimann, Jim, and Rip Georges. *California Crazy, Roadside Vernacular Architecture.* San Francisco: Chronicle Books, 1980.

Hess, Alan. *Googie, Fifties Coffee Shop Architecture.* San Francisco: Chronicle Books, 1985.

"Highways are Happy Ways." *American Restaurant* 37 (May 1954) 124–125.

"Highway Restaurants" *Architectural Record* (October 1954): 163, 167–169.

Hirshorn, Paul, and Stephen Izenour. "White Towers." Cambridge, Massachusetts: The MIT Press, 1979.

Hooker, Richard J. *Food and Drink in America: A History.* Indianapolis, Indiana: The Bobbs-Merrill Company, 1981.

Hoopes, Lydia Clawson. "From Root Beer Stand to Millions." *American Restaurant* 21 (May 1938): 39.

"Hot Doges De Luxe." *Woman's Home Companion* (March 1930): 4.

"Houston's Drive-In Trade Gets Girl Show With Its Hamburgers." *Life* (February 26, 1940): 84–87.

"The Howard Johnson's Restaurants." *Fortune* 22 (September 1940): 82–87, 94, 96.

"How's Business with Diners?" *American Restaurant* 31 (February 1949): 120–125.

"How Drive-Ins Compare With Other Restaurants." *Drive-In Restaurant* 32 (April 1968): 40.

"How Pig Stands Started the Drive-In Restaurant." *Drive-In Management* (September 1961): 22–30.

Huxtable, Ada Louise. "Architecture for a Fast Food Culture." *New York Times Magazine* (February 12, 1978): 23–25.

Iggers, Jeremy. "The Band Box, Where the Little Rhythms of Life Are Played Out Every Day." *The Minneapolis Star Tribune Sunday Magazine* (July 24, 1988): 6–11.

Ingram, E. W., Sr. *All This From a 5-cent Hamburger! The Story of the White Castle System.* New York: The Newcomen Society in North America, 1964.

Jackson, Donald Dale. "The American Diner is in Decline, Yet More Chic Than Ever." *Smithsonian* (1973): 94–101.

Jewell, Derek. *Man and Motor: The 20th Century Love Affair.* New York: Walker and Company, 1966.

Jones, Dwayne, and Roni Morales. "Pig Stands, The Beginning of the Drive-In Restaurant." *SCA News Journal* 12 (Winter 1991–92): 2–5.

Jones, Evan. *American Food: The Gastronomic Story.* New York: Dutton, 1975.

Kaplan, Donald, and Alan Bellink. *Classic Diners of the Northeast.* Boston, Massachusetts: Faber and Faber, 1980.

Karshner, Roger. *Working Class Monologues.* Toluca Lake, California: Dramaline Publications, 1988.

Keller, Ulrich. *The Highway as Habitat: A Roy Stryker Documentation, 1943–1955.* Santa Barbara, California: University Art Museum, 1986.

Kendall, Elaine. "The Most Famous Boring Food In America." *Vogue* (October 1, 1969): 258, 260–261, 265.

Kerber, Ross. "Rare Old Trolleys Are Really Piling Up in Kennebunkport." *The Wall Street Journal* (September 16, 1997): 1.

Kerr, Peter. "Chrome Walls and Formica Do Not Just a Diner Make." *The New York Times* (November 29, 1990): B1.

Kittel, Gerd. *Diners: People and Places.* New York, New York: Thames and Hudson Inc., 1990.

Knight, Jerry. "To Giaimo, the Old Diner Concept Has a Silver Lining." *The Washington Post* 118 (April 1, 1996): 27.

Kroc, Ray, with Robert Anderson. *Grinding It Out: The Making of McDonald's.* Chicago, Illinois: Henry Regnery Company, 1977.

Kullman Dining Car Company. Various Corporate Brochures and Sales Literature (circa 1930s to 1950s).

Kuralt, Charles. *A Life on the Road.* New York: Ivy Books, published by Ballantine Books, 1990.

Kurtz, Stephen A. *Wasteland: Building the American Dream.* New York: Praeger Publishers, 1973.

Langdon, Philip. *Orange Roofs, Golden Arches: The Architecture of American Chain Restaurants.* New York: Alfred A. Knopf, 1986.

Lender, Mark Edward, and James K. Martin. *Drinking in America: A History.* New York: The Free Press, 1982.

Lent, Henry B. *The Automobile-U.S.A.: Its Impact on Peoples' Lives and the National Economy.* New York: E. P. Dutton and Company Inc., 1968.

Levinson, Barry. *Diner* [screenplay]. Santa Monica, California: Citron Manuscripts [distributor], [198-].

Lewis, David L., and Lawrence Goldstein. *The Automobile and American Culture.* Ann Arbor, Michigan: The University of Michigan Press, 1980.

Liddle, Alan. "Mels Drive-In Captures the Style of the Fifties." *Restaurant News* 21: 2 (January 5, 1987): 1.

Liebs, Chester. *Main Street to Miracle Mile: American Roadside Architecture.* Boston: Little, Brown and Company, 1985.

Lipin, David. "Ben Frank's to Reopen as Mels." *West Hollywood Independent* 74 (April 23, 1997): 1, 3.

"Lunch Wagons De Luxe." *Christian Science Monitor* (March 23, 1938): 14.

The Little Rascals, Volume 10; *The Lucky Corner.* Hal Roach Studios Inc.: Cabin Fever Entertainment, 1994.

Love, John F. *McDonald's: Behind the Arches.* New York: Bantam Books, 1986.

"Lunch Wagons Streamline—Customers Stream In." *Nation's Business* 25 (September 1937): 74.

Lundegaard, Karen. "$14M Deal Puts Diner Chain on NASDAQ Menu." *Washington Business Journal* 14:46 (March 29, 1996): 1, 36.

Luxenberg, Stan. *Roadside Empires: How the Chains Franchised America.* New York: Viking Penguin Inc., 1985.

Makarewicz, Julie. "To Fry For: Diner's Exodus From Jersey is Over Easy." *The Grand Rapids Press* (October 5, 1995): B1.

Maguire, Gregory. *The Peace and Quiet Diner.* New York: Parents Magazine Press; Milwaukee: G. Stevens, 1994.

Mariani, John. *America Eats Out: An Illustrated History of Restaurants, Coffee Shops, Speakeasies, and Other Establishments that Have Fed Us for 350 Years.* New York: William Morrow and Company Inc., 1991.

Marling, Karal Ann. *The Colossus of Roads: Myth and Symbol Along the American Highway.* Minneapolis: University of Minnesota Press, 1984.

Marshall, J. "Those Diner Blues." *Collier's* 113 (February 12, 1944): 21.

Martinez, Barbara. "Would You Like to Hear About the Specials? Then Read This Poll." *The Wall Street Journal* (September 23, 1997).

Martin, P. "Roadside Business: Casualty of War." *The Saturday Evening Post* 215 (August 8, 1942): 16–17.

Matteson, Donald W. *The Auto Radio, A Romantic Genealogy.* Jackson, Michigan: Thornridge Publishing, 1987.

McKay, Betsy. "Meatloaf With a Russian Twist, Muscovites Line up for Down-Home Cooking at the Starlite Diner." *The Dallas Morning News* (March 2, 1996): 2C, 3C.

Mozzocco, Edward A. "The Diner That Wouldn't Give Up." *American Restaurant* 32 (January 1950): 34.

Munroe, Charles C. "When You Buy an Electric Sign—." *American Restaurant* 7 (December 1924): 42.

National Trust for Historic Preservation. *Ducks and Diners.* Edited by Diane Maddex and Janet Walker, Washington, D.C.: The Preservation Press, 1988.

"The New Outlet—Roadside Refreshment Stands." *Printer's Ink* 135 (April 22, 1926): 127.

"New Space Age Design." Sales Brochure, Kullman Dining Car Company, Inc. (circa 1960s).

"Off the Highways." *Business Week* (June 19, 1943): 60.

Offitzer, Karen. *Diners.* New York: Metro Books, Friedman/Fairfax Publishers, 1997.

"One Hundred Truckers Stop Her Daily." *American Restaurant* 39 (July 1956): 67.

"One Million Hamburgers and 160 Tons of French Fries a Year." *American Restaurant* (July 1952): 44–45.

"Palaces of the Hot Doges." *Architectural Forum* 63 (August 1935): 30–31.

"Pal's Diner Opens in Michigan." *The Reporter*. Mahwah, New Jersey (30 August 1996): 1.

Pearce, Christopher. *Fifties Sourcebook: A Visual Guide to the Style of a Decade*. Secaucus, New Jersey: Chartwell Books, 1990.

Pearl's Diner. A Film by Lynn Smith, National Film Board of Canada. Morris Plains, New Jersey: Lucerne Media, 1982.

Pearson, John. "For an Aficionado, A Diner is More Than a Food Joint." *The Wall Street Journal* (December 13, 1989): 1, A7.

"Pick a Good Location." *American Restaurant Magazine* (October 1954): 71–73.

Pillsbury, Richard. *From Boarding House to Bistro: American Restaurants Then and Now*. Cambridge, Massachusetts: Unwin Hyman, 1990.

"Postwar Dining Cars Will Feature Diagonal Arrangement of Tables." *Scientific American* 172 (January 1945): 38.

"Ptomaine Joe's Place." *Collier's* 102 (October 1, 1938): 54.

The Purple Rose of Cairo. Jack Rollings and Charles H. Joffee Productions and Orion Pictures Corporation. Los Angeles, California. Orion Home Video, 1995.

"Quick Lunch in California, Kenneth Bemis and his Sixty-Two Imitation Pioneer Log Cabins." *Fortune* 18 (July 1937): 4.

Rapoport, Roger. "Restored Soda Fountains of Yesterday." *Americana* 19 (July–August 1991): 60–61, 64.

Rice, Dana. "The Lunch Wagon Settles Down." *New York Times Magazine* (October 19, 1941): 20.

"Roadside Diners for Motorists." *The Architectural Record* 76 (July 1934): 56–57.

"The Roadside Stand Grows Up—Ultra Modern, Magnificent." *Drive-In Restaurant and Highway Cafe Magazine* (November 1955): 21, 27.

Rockland, Michael Aaron. "The Rest of America May Belong to the Fast-Food Chains, but New Jersey is Proud to be Its Diner Capital," *New Jersey Monthly* (October 1977): 53–59.

Rodd, W. C. "One Building for Two Types of Clientele." *American Restaurant Magazine* (August 1948): 35–37, 131.

"Rolling Restaurants; Trailer Food Trucks." *Business Week* (April 1942): 78.

Root, Waverley, and Richard de Rochement. *Eating in America: A History*. New York: William Morrow and Company, 1976.

Rubin, Charles J., David Rollert, John Farago, and Jonathan Etra. *Junk Food*. New York: Dell Publishing Company Inc., 1980.

Ryan, Michael. "A Diner That Delivers Good Kids." *Parade Magazine* (March 27, 1994): 14.

Sargeant, Winthrop. "Roadside Restaurant." *Life* 31 (August 13, 1931): 75–76.

Scala, Ted. "Diner Redux." *Spirit* (July 1995): 48–52.

Scharf, Virginia. *Taking the Wheel: Women and the Coming of the Motor Age*. Albuquerque, New Mexico: University of New Mexico Press, 1992

"Sell Passers-by With Smarter Fronts." *American Restaurant* 36 (September 1953): 62–63.

"75 Years of Foodservice History." *Restaurant Business* 75 (May 1976): 43–44.

Silk, Gerald, Angelo Anselmi, Henry Robert Jr., and Strother MacMinn. *Automobile and Culture*. New York: Harry N. Abrams Inc., 1984.

Silver Diner. *American Diner History*. Unpublished Company Literature. Rockville, Maryland: Silver Diner Inc., 1997.

Silverman, Chip; foreword by Barry Levinson. *Diner Guys*. New York, New York: Carol Publishing Group, 1989.

Skidmore, H. B. "Open Day and Night: Silver Line Diner, Jersey City." *Woman's Journal* 13 (1928): 22.

"'Slice of Pie and a Cup of Coffee—That'll be Fifteen Cents, Honey.'" *American Heritage* 28 (April 1977): 68–71.

Smith, Mark, and Naomi Black. *America on Wheels: Tales and Trivia of the Automobile*. New York: William Morrow and Company Inc., 1986.

Society for Commercial Archeology Inc. *All Night, All-Night Diner Tour*. Boston, Massachusetts: Society for Commercial Archeology, April 1980.

The Automobile in Design and Culture. Edited by Jan Jennings. Ames: Iowa State University Press, 1990.

Society for Commercial Archeology News Journal. Volume 1, Number 1 through Volume 15, Number 2. (September 1978 through Fall 1997).

S.C.A. News. Volume 1, Number 1 through Volume 5, Number 3. (Spring 1993 through Fall 1997).

Soule, Gardner B. "The Old Dog Wagon Puts on the Dog." *Popular Science* 162 (March 1953): 138–141.

Staal, Michele. "Famous Diner Makes its Way to Cascade Shopping Center." *ADA/Forest Hills Advance* 27:39 (October 4, 1995): 1.

Stern, Jane, and Michael Stern. *A Taste of America*. New York: Andrews and McMeel, 1988.

RoadFood. New York: HarperCollins Publishers Inc., 1992.

"Streamlined Restaurants Will Not Sell Tomorrow's Customers." *Drive-In Restaurant and Highway Cafe Magazine* 19 (June 1955): 9.

Taylor, F. J. "This Burger Business." *Collier's* (January 25, 1941): 107:22.

Tennyson, Jeffrey. *Hamburger Heaven: The Illustrated History of the Hamburger*. New York: Hyperion, 1993.

Tinsley, Jesse. "2 Vintage Diners Will Soon Call Lee Road Home." *The Cleveland Plain Dealer* (December 2, 1996): 1-B and 2-B.

Tompkins, Raymond S. "Hash-House Visionaries." *The American Mercury* 22 (March 1931): 361.

Upton, Robert J. "Rural Diners Serve up a Heaping Helping of Backroads Flavor." *New Mexico Magazine* (March 1994): 56–59.

Waiting for the Light. Epic Productions and Sarlui/Diamant presents and Edward R. Pressman Production. Burbank, California: RCA/Columbia Pictures Home Video, 1991.

Watts, Gilbert S. *Roadside Marketing*. New York: Orange Judd Publishing Company Inc., 1928.

"When the Lunch Wagon Made its Bow." *New York Times Magazine* (February 7, 1926): 20.

"Where Do We Eat?" *Ladies Home Journal* 51 (May 1934): 133.

Wilkins, Mike; Ken Smith, and Doug Kirby. *The New Updated and Expanded Roadside America*. New York: Simon and Schuster, 1986.

"Will the Postwar Restaurant Look Like This?" *American Restaurant* 25 (June 1943): 46.

Wilson, Richard Guy; Dianne H. Pilgrim, and Dickran Tashjian. *The Machine Age in America 1918–1941*. New York: Harry N. Abrams Inc., 1986.

Witzel, Michael Karl. *The American Drive-In: History and Folklore of the Drive-In Restaurant in American Car Culture*. Osceola, Wisconsin: MBI Publishing Company, 1994.

Drive-In Deluxe. Osceola, Wisconsin: MBI Publishing Company, 1997.

Route 66 Remembered. Osceola, Wisconsin: MBI Publishing Company, 1996.

Cruisin': Car Culture in America. Osceola, Wisconsin: MBI Publishing Company, 1997.

Wood, Paul. "Local Landmark Diner Takes Trip Cross Country." *The Ridgewood News* (October 3, 1996): 2.

Woodson, Leroy Jr. *Roadside Food*. New York: Stewart, Tabori, and Chang Inc., 1986.

"Workers Lunch Wagon." *Business Week* (May 31, 1941): 30.

Worthington, Diane Rossen. *Diner: The Best of Casual American Cooking*. Menlo Park, California: Sunset Publishing, 1995.

Young, Andrew D. *Trolley to the Past: A Brief History and Companion to the Operating Trolley Museums of North America*. Glendale, California: Interurban Press, 1983.

Young, Marilynn. "Drive-In to Take Over at Ben Frank's." *Westside Weekly* (August 10, 1997): 6.

Young-Witzel, Gyvel, and Michael Karl Witzel. *Soda Pop! From Miracle Medicine to Pop Culture*. Stillwater, Minnesota: Voyageur Press, 1997.

INDEX